SOVIETICA

PUBLICATIONS

OF THE INSTITUTE OF EAST-EUROPEAN STUDIES

UNIVERSITY OF FRIBOURG / SWITZERLAND

Edited by

J. M. BOCHEŃSKI

STUDIES IN SOVIET THOUGHT

I

STUDIES

IN SOVIET THOUGHT

I

Edited by J. M. Bocheński and T. J. Blakeley

D. REIDEL PUBLISHING COMPANY / DORDRECHT-HOLLAND

TABLE OF CONTENTS

PREFACE

Early in 1958 a number of research projects on Soviet philosophy were started at the Institute of East-European Studies at the University of Fribourg (Switzerland) under the direction of the undersigned. At present, they are all completed or nearly so and their results are described in 18 different volumes. In spite of the fact that all of them have been already published or soon will be (mostly in German), it has been thought worthwhile to present their main conclusions in the form of short English reports.

This book contains in the main these reports. Only the two programmatic papers (my own and that of Dr. Buchholz) and the study of Dr. Dahm are not direct results of the above-mentioned projects. But it will be clear to everyone that they, too, are closely connected with the subject envisaged and are written from a similar point of view.

It will, perhaps, be convenient to briefly formulate this standpoint. All the writings included here are concerned with *recent* (i.e. mainly post-Stalinist) developments in *Soviet philosophy*, where "Soviet" is taken in the wide meaning of the word, covering also Marxism-Leninism in Communist countries other than the Soviet Union. All the authors started with the assumption that there are *interesting aspects* to these more recent developments. There was also a common assumption that only *specialized* work on *first-hand sources* can be of relevance in this field. In short, it is the editor's belief that the main methodological views stated in his programmatic paper ("On Soviet Studies") were uniformly held by the authors.

Each of them worked independently and carries, therefore, complete responsibility for his contribution to this volume. This does not mean, however, that there was no contact and even close collaboration between the writers. On the contrary, if the results presented here could be obtained, this was due for a large part to close contact and continuous exchange of information between most of the writers. To this team-work are due, among others, such auxiliary productions of the Institute as the two issues of the Bibliography (see "A Bibliography of Soviet Philosophy"), my own *"Einführung"* and *"Grundlagen"*, as also Prof. Lobkowicz's book on contradictions (see his article on the subject). It is the belief of the undersigned that each of the papers here published by his colleagues brings new insights and information on phenomena which were and still are very little known. But, in addition to these scientific results, one practical conclusion has been established beyond any doubt – that such team-work is of paramount importance in Sovietological studies. It can only be hoped that the Fribourg team, which seems to have been the first and as yet the only group devoted to research in recent Soviet philosophy, will not remain unique in the future. For we still know very little and a tremendous effort is needed in order to reach a genuine understanding of contemporary Soviet thought.

I am under the pleasant obligation to express my thanks to all the authors for their collaboration, more especially to Dr. Buchholz and Dr. Dahm for their permission to include their respective articles in this book. I am very much obliged to Dr. Blakeley, who acted as managing editor of the volume and translated most of the papers. Last but not least, thanks are due to the Rockefeller Foundation, whose generous grant made the studies of about half of the present writers possible.

J. M. BOCHEŃSKI

CONTRIBUTORS

T. Blakeley, Ph. D. (USA), Assistant-Professor, Institute of East-European Studies at the University of Fribourg (Switzerland).

J. M. Bocheński, Ph. D. S.T.D. (Switzerland), Professor of the History of Contemporary Philosophy and Director of the Institute of East-European Studies at the University of Fribourg (Switzerland).

A. Buchholz, Ph. D. (Germany), Editor of "Osteuropa-Naturwissenschaft", Stuttgart, Germany.

H. Dahm, Ph. D. (Germany), Editor of "Ost-Probleme", Bonn, Germany.

H. Fleischer, Ph. D. (Germany), Institute of East-European Studies at the University of Fribourg (Switzerland).

Z. Jordan, Ph. D. (Poland), Institute of East-European Studies at the University of Fribourg (Switzerland).

G. Küng (Switzerland), Institute of East-European Studies at the University of Fribourg (Switzerland).

N. Lobkowicz, Ph. D. (Czechoslovakia), Associate Professor, University of Notre Dame, Indiana, USA.

S. Müller-Markus, Ph. D. (Germany), Institute of East-European Studies at the University of Fribourg (Switzerland).

L. Vrtačič, M.A. (Jugoslavia), Institute of East-European Studies at the University of Fribourg (Switzerland).

J. M. BOCHEŃSKI

ON SOVIET STUDIES

The aim of this paper is to present some characteristics and problems of Sovietology, especially as concerned with Communist *thought*, i.e. with ideology. Sovietology is, in fact, a young discipline, and many incorrect notions about it are circulated not only among the general public but even among scholars.

What is Sovietology? It may briefly be described as the science concerned with Communism *as such*. In every Communist country there are, of course, other factors influencing development and a Sovietologist must take them into account. But his main and central interest is not these other factors. He is interested in Communism. It follows that the "Soviet" in "Sovietology" does not denote the Soviet Union alone; there is, for example, now a discipline called "Sinosovietology" which studies Chinese Communism; and happenings in Poland or Jugoslavia are also legitimate subjects of Sovietology in so far as they are considered from the point of view of Communist influence.

One may ask why such a science is necessary. Is it not enough to have normal, say, Slavic or Sinological studies? After all, the Communist period in the life of such countries as Bulgaria or China is most certainly but one period of their history; and there seems to be no peculiar reason for having a special science for this one period. Yet Sovietology *is* necessary. The main reason for it is, that Communism is not only a national factor in each country in which it took the power, but also and above all, an international movement with very peculiar, perhaps unique, characteristics. One instance may perhaps clarify what we mean. If we take China we shall find, of course, that the understanding of its contemporary history is not possible without a serious knowledge of Chinese language, geography, history, culture, and so on. Yet, all that together will not be enough if one wishes to really understand the phenomena at hand; for its history is being made now, in the frame of the old Chinese culture, etc., by a new and powerful factor, the Chinese Communist Party. Now this

1

party is, in spite of all that might be original and Chinese in it, still a *Communist* Party. It has the same creed, the same organization, the same type of institutions and the same fundamental rules of behaviour as other Communist parties. That is why a *mere* Sinologist, i.e. one who does not know these specific factors, is not able to understand the happenings.

But, as Communism develops in each country in a somewhat different way, there will be two parts to Sovietology. On the one hand, we shall have *General Sovietology*, the study of what is *common* to all Communist parties and countries. On the other, there will be a number of *special Sovietologies*, devoted to the peculiar realizations of Communism in each country or group of countries. General Sovietology will be the basic discipline for each of the latter; a student of, say, Hungarian Communism will have to be, first of all, well-trained in it, and then only will he study Hungarian language, history, culture, etc. Because of the priority of General Sovietology we shall here be concerned with it above all.

But even General Sovietology is not a science which could possibly be studied without a due consideration of the concrete materializations of Communism, or, more precisely, of one such materialization. Communism in general, as it is now, is mainly the work of Lenin and his followers who were Russians, and it was in Russia that Communism first took root. Up to today, in spite of the growth of other parties, the Communist Party of the Soviet Union (which is the old Russian Communist Party) is still considered by all of them as the leader and model. Both in regard to creed and to organization, every Communist Party adheres, as to the essentials, to the standards of the Soviet Communist Party. Therefore, General Sovietology is to a very large extent the study of Russian or (more recently) Soviet Communism.

What sort of study will it be? It is not easy to classify this science into the accepted scheme of disciplines because it embraces such widely different subjects. Communism is a philosophy in action and a knowledge of the History of Philosophy is, obviously, a prerequisite for its understanding; it is a political movement and only a political scientist is fit to grasp it; it rose out of certain historical circumstances which are studied by the historian; it acts powerfully on human society and is, in turn, conditioned by it – thus it seems to fall into the field of sociology.

2

And the same could be said of nearly every other human science, e.g., political economy has, clearly, also much to say in this domain. If we consider, however, the fundamental structure of Communism, we shall find that there are two sciences which could claim more than any other the right of being competent in the domain. First of all, Communism is a philosophic doctrine, purporting to state the most general laws of being and development. It originated with such philosophers as Marx, Engels, Lenin. Clearly, philosophy and the history of philosophy are most relevant here. On the other hand, Communism is an organization; as such it falls into the field of sociology. It may be said that a Sovietologist must be, in any case, either a philosopher or a sociologist, but, best of all, both. Anyway, he should have a good training in at least one of these disciplines and an understanding of the other.

Yet that is not all. The field covered by General Sovietology (and the same is true of each special Sovietology) is an enormous one. No single scholar is able to know all of it in a scientific way. For example, the literature of a Communist country is surely an important aspect of its life; but, in order to know it, one must be a specialist in literary studies. The economy of a Communist country is not only an important aspect of its life, but is also strictly connected with Communism as such. But economy can be correctly understood only by an economist. Similar remarks can be made about many other aspects.

It follows, that General Sovietology will have to be subdivided into a *basic part*, which must be known by every scholar working in the field, and *special sectors*. The basic part comprehends, among others, at least the following topics:

Russian language
Russian history
Marxism
History of the Russian (and Soviet) Communist Party
Leninism and its development after Lenin
Organization and institutions of the Party.

One who would like to devote himself to special studies in Sovietology, either general or special, has to acquire knowledge in these fields. After that, he will study his own department, e.g. Soviet or Chinese or Polish economy, nationality problem, art, religion, etc. If he does not work directly on Soviet problems, he will still have to be in touch with them

3

– thus, one who studies agriculture, say, in Eastern Germany, will have to know agricultural developments in the Soviet Union, and the same is true of other fields.

We can now outline the *curriculum* a Sovietologist has to follow in order that he be sufficiently prepared for research.
He has *first* to acquire a training in his own field – e.g. in philosophy, sociology, history, law, economy, etc. This must be a *full* university training, terminated at least by an M.A., better by a Ph. D. This will supply him not only with the knowledge and methods of the specific field he has chosen but also with a general preparation for scientific work. *Then* he has to undergo a training in basic General Sovietology, i.e. in the topics enumerated above. If he is not a philosopher or sociologist by his earlier studies, he will, in the course of this second period, also learn at least the ABC of these disciplines. This second training takes, as experience has shown, an average of three years. If the first preparation was solid and the future Sovietologist is a serious worker, he will be able, during the three years, not only to acquire the necessary basic knowledge, but also to produce a contribution toward the progress of Sovietology in some limited sector.
In the *third* place, he can devote himself to the study of a special Sovietology. He will be able to anticipate such studies already during the second period; but it is only after the completion of that period that he will be able to devote himself entirely to his chosen country or group of countries.
The above program may seem to be very harsh and exacting. As a matter of fact, it is not an easy road to follow; and that is the reason why we have so few Sovietologists worthy of the name, and why the value of *most* things written about Communism is so questionable. It must, however, be emphasized that there is *no other way* of acquiring the necessary skills and knowledge. In particular, two dangerous mistakes must be indicated in this respect.
One would be tempted to think that a specialist in one classical discipline – e.g. an economist – could without a training in Sovietology understand whatever happens in Communist countries. The second would be to believe that somebody who knows, e.g., Russian or Serb and knows those countries also otherwise (their history, etc.), can grasp, say, the economic phenomena without being himself an economist. *Two* trainings

4

are necessary: the general (here, economics) and the special (Soviet-ological).

I shall now consider some problems of one of the central Sovietological disciplines, namely of the study of Communist thought, above all of Communist philosophy. The main problems here are concerned with the temporal delimitation of the subject. It seems to me that there is a lot of misunderstanding in this respect and that a clear statement of the question is urgently needed.

Communist thought has a history of more than a century. It originated with Karl Marx, was developed by Lenin and is still developing since his death. If we consider this long evolution, we shall be struck by the fact that during these 120 years or so, Communist philosophy was developing under widely different conditions and in the frame of widely different mental settings. It is easy to indicate the three main phases of that development – I shall call them for convenience the "Marxian", the "Leninist" and the "Soviet" periods; and what was or is produced during them, I shall call respectively "Marxism", "Leninism" and "contemporary Soviet thought".

(1) MARXISM. Let us consider the background out of which Marx's doctrines arose. We have, first, the industrial revolution at about 1850 in Western Europe. Then we have German Philosophy, or rather that peculiar sort of German philosophy with which Marx was acquainted in his youth – the thought of, say, Bruno Bauer, Ludwig Feuerbach, Max Stirner, and so on. We must then take into consideration the personality of Karl Marx – a fertile and sometimes powerful thinker. Marxism is the product of the conditions existing in Western Europe about 1850, of German philosophy of the same time, and of Karl Marx's own genius.

These conditions being rather unique in history and Karl Marx himself being most certainly an original thinker, it would be good to reserve the word "Marxism" for *his own* thought, or at most, for his own thought plus that of Engels. Anyway, the study of that thought requires a peculiar training and a specific type of knowledge. There is a special scientific discipline, called *"Marxology"*, which deals with such problems. I would like to make a plea for the autonomy of that discipline. It seems clear to me that knowledge of Lenin or of post-Leninist thinkers – who are all from radically different milieus — is of little avail for the understanding of Karl Marx. On the other hand, a Marxologist has no competence at all to deal, say, with the doctrines of Lenin or Stalin. Marxology is not Sovietology.

However, a Sovietologist must be interested in Marxology. For, while Leninism and what followed had no influence on Marxism, Marxism itself did influence Leninism and the later Soviet doctrines. This may be formulated in the following statement: Marxology is an auxiliary science for Sovietology, but not inversely.

(2) LENINISM. Next, we have to do with Lenin. The conditions in which he was educated and in which he formed his doctrines are very different from those in which Marx lived and thought. For these conditions are the well-known situation in the Russia of about 1900 – a backward country with traditions and institutions totally different from those of the England and Germany of 1850. Moreover, the spiritual background of Lenin is radically different from that of Marx. It will be enough to quote such names as Belinskij, Černyševskij, Nečaev, Tkačev, and Ogarev, to realize this. And, then again, Lenin is a personal thinker of great creative power. He most certainly took over a lot from Marx (and, unfortunately, also from Engels) – but practically everything he accepted was transformed by him, in virtue of his quite different background and quite different personality. Some elements, like practically all of the doctrines of the "young" Marx, were simply dropped. Some others, like economic determinism, were profoundly altered. And many new doctrines were formulated.

We have here, therefore, a new field of research. The worker in this field must have a special training and possess a lot of knowledge which is quite irrelevant, or nearly so, to a Marxologist. He must, for example, understand pretty well the Russian thought before Lenin; he must know the conditions in which Lenin developed his doctrine, and so on.

As in the case of Marxism, I would again venture to claim autonomy for this field and its science, *Leninology*. I mean by this not only the study of Lenin, but also of his milieu (of such men as Bucharin and Trotsky, etc.) – viz. up to the death of Lenin and the great purges of the 1930's which liquidated the men and ended the period.

And I would say that a Leninologist must know Marxism, and that a Sovietologist must be, of course, interested in Leninology, which is to him a very important auxiliary science, but not inversely. As the Marxologist, so the pure Leninologist is incompetent as regards recent Soviet phenomena, even if he is nearer to them than the former.

(3) CONTEMPORARY SOVIET THOUGHT. Then the third period arises. The conditions have changed – a great industrial civilization is formed. With it, the type of thinker changes also. The most important among them are no longer amateurish demagogues and writers – they are technicians. The background of Soviet thought is constituted more and more by the great universities in which technical, naturalist thinking is dominant. No name can be attached to this period and to the new factors marking it – certainly not that of Stalin, who simply continued Leninism, as far as doctrines are concerned, even if he did contribute somewhat to the change in his last years (1947 and 1950), and less still Khrushchov or another of the contemporary leaders, who seem to be far less important as thinkers than Marx and Lenin. But a new period is certainly in the making. This new period is not marked by a complete break with the preceding one; to think so – and perhaps most of the dilettantes writing in Sovietology do think in this way – is to completely ignore Soviet reality and one of the major laws of historical development. The new Soviet thought takes over Leninism, drops something from it, transforms other elements and adds still new ones – exactly as Lenin did with Marxism. Moreover, the new period is by far not yet established. Most of the ruling men in the Soviet Union – and still more in the other Communist countries – belong completely to the second period; they are not scientifically trained technicians, but politicians with little understanding of science. Yet something new is growing. This can be not only predicted from the general conditions, but also shown in some detail, which is the object of this book.

It is again my opinion that the study of contemporary Soviet thought is an autonomous discipline. It must, obviously, rely on Marxology and Leninology; but a Sovietologist in this meaning of the word need not be either a Marxologist or a Leninologist. Of course, he will have to know Lenin's thought, but the more subtle questions of Leninology – for example, the problems of the relations between Lenin and Bucharin – are of no importance for him. Less still need he know what Karl Marx thought at such and such a period and what were the influences acting on him at a certain time. He is no more competent in these disciplines than the students of Marx or Lenin are in his. Sovietology has its own enormous field and requires specialization.

It seems that practice fully confirms these views. We, fortunately, do have some good Marxologists and Leninologists and we use their works. Whoever knows them will realize that they are moving in regions different from those of the Sovietologist. Moreover, it will be evident to him that a normal person has no possibility of mastering, at the same time, these three very large fields. This may be regrettable, but it is so. As in many other departments of science, we are bound to specialize if we are to achieve anything of real importance.

Sovietology is a *very* difficult field of research. At the same time, it is a discipline which shares with Indology and a few other sciences the highly questionable privilege of being loved by a large crowd of dilettantes and cranks. Who is not interested in Communism and in the Soviet Union? Hundreds, if not thousands, of people who do not understand a word of Russian, who do not know even the ABC of the subject and of its methods, are constantly writing and talking about it. They may be divided into the following classes:

(a) Scholars, specialized in some discipline, but without Sovietological training,

(b) Marxologists not specialized in the 20th century and in Communism,

(c) Ex-Communists without any scientific training at all,

(d) People who have been in the Soviet Union or in another Communist country, but lack scientific knowledge in the field,

(e) Politicians, newspapermen, clergymen and other people who cannot even claim the little knowledge possessed by the preceding groups.

Of course, members of each of these classes can sometimes produce valuable materials – above all, those listed under (c) and (d). But it should be emphasized that whatever they offer are *materials* for scientific enquiry and little more. Let us take one instance: somebody has been imprisoned in a Soviet Labour Camp for a number of years and then released. What he has to say is of interest, if he is a good and impartial observer – which is by no means always the case. But if the same man purports to make a synthesis of the problem and to state conclusions concerning the system of labour camps as a whole, his work will be valueless unless he is, at the same time, a trained Sovietologist and has the needed materials at his disposal. As a matter of fact, we now have about 100,000 testimonies of people who have been, at various times, in such labour camps. There is also a literature of more than 50 volumes of memoirs. All this has been already elaborated – for example, by Mora Zwierniak, Dallin-Nikolayevski and Barton; most of the authors have never been in a Soviet camp, but there is no doubt that, using an ample material and elaborating it by scientific methods, they were able to give far more and far better information than *any* of the authors of memoirs based on personal experience only.

Now, the fact that some people write unscientific books might be thought to be irrelevant. Unfortunately, it is not. If the authors enjoy a certain authority – and often they do, as ambassadors, scientists, former prominent Communists, etc. – they will be easily believed. The very status of Sovietology is made uncertain by this fact. Tremendous financial and human resources, which could have been usefully applied to scientific research, are wasted on dilettante productions. This is a great difficulty with which our science meets daily.

Yet it may be called an exterior difficulty. After all, the nonsense written down by others cannot seriously harm the research from inside even if it creates difficulties for it from the outside. But for Sovietology there is no lack of internal difficulties.

There is, first, the nature of the sources. It is well-known that the degree of interpretation needed in order to use a Soviet source is far greater than what is usual. One instance is statistics. Sometimes – as in the case of Gerschenkron – long and arduous work was needed to get anything from the figures contained in the sources. But not only statistics are suspect. The following instance of a blunder committed by the writer of the present paper shows how difficult it sometimes is to understand what is going on.

In 1951 two men, a certain Majstrov and Prof. Tugarinov, violently attacked Prof. Janovskaja, a serious worker in formal logic. The objections they formulated were of such a low level and sometimes so obviously nonsensical that it should have been clear to everyone that two reactionaries were trying to stop the progress accomplished by Prof. Janovskaja. This is what I wrote at the time. But I learned from Prof. Janovskaja herself that Tugarinov is one of her pupils. A study of his work was made at the same time by Dr. Fleischer, who found that, far from being a

9

reactionary, he was one of the most progressive and scientific minds in contemporary Soviet philosophy. How on earth, then, could he write such barbaric nonsense against his master? Well, the answer might be this: at a certain time the school of Prof. Janovskaja decided that the situation was dangerous and that some "self-criticism" was needed to save the day. Tugarinov was designated to operate that self-criticism by insulting Prof. Janovskaja, his teacher, and his science at the same time. That was all.

One problem with which a Sovietologist meets every day may be formulated as follows: how far does a Soviet philosopher believe what he writes? Mr. Blakeley made a rather thorough study of one of the leaders in Soviet philosophy, Prof. Kedrov. He found that Kedrov was constantly changing not only his attitude but even his theses. Now, Prof. Kedrov is certainly no coward. He showed great courage under Stalin when he was chief editor of the *"Voprosy filosofii"* in 1947 and 1948. He is also a quite distinguished personal thinker. And yet he sometimes writes things which he simply cannot believe.

Or, as an instance of the opposite, take the case of the late Prof. Rubinštejn. Nobody can doubt that he was a distinguished scholar and personal thinker. His "Principles of General Psychology" contain a well thought-out general view of the human complex. But after 1950 (the year in which Soviet psychologists "decided" to become Pavlovian) he recanted his views, and this in such an intelligent and coherent way that I can simply find no other explanation than that he really changed his mind. But did he really?

Another difficulty which Sovietology encounters is caused by the tremendous pace of development in Soviet philosophy. Something new is certainly rising – a new generation, and one with a training and mentality very different from that of the former, is now beginning to publish. If one follows, e.g., the *"Voprosy filosofii"* one will find that every year, nearly in every issue, there is something new – not only in details but even, I would say, in the general attitude. A great break-through was constituted by the articles of Kedrov, Kamenskij and Markov in 1947/48. Another is the paper of A.D. Aleksandrov of 1958. A third is the famous discussion on contradictions in the same year (Prof. Lobkowicz describes its results in this volume). These are only a few instances out of the large number which might have been quoted.

Last but not least, the handicap rising from practical considerations –
moral and political bias – must be mentioned. Communism is now of
vital importance for practically every man, above all if he is a man who
thinks. Moreover, it appears not only as a physical threat but also as a
spiritual challenge. It is not only difficult, it is simply impossible, not to
take a stand in regard to it. And it is the conviction of the present writer
that this is legitimate – one has the right and even the duty to take a
stand in this context.

But there is a wide-spread opinion to the effect that such a stand, once
assumed, influences research. Therefore, already *a priori*, there seems to
be no place for a *neutral, objective* study of the field. This is, in fact, what
the Communists themselves affirm. Experience teaches us that there is
very little objective Sovietology – what we find in this domain is biased
either by enthusiasm or by aversion for Communism.

Nevertheless, impartial study in Sovietology *is* possible. For one thing,
it is a fact that even if the class of serious writers in this domain is small,
it is still not an empty class. The existence of objective Sovietology is a
fact; and *ab esse ad posse valet illatio.*

It seems, moreover, that the above-mentioned view on the possibility of
objectivity is not true. I think that it is the result of an over-emphasis
on the animal factor in man. It supposes that man is not capable of rising
above his instincts and passions – that he cannot hold an impartial view
where his profound moral or physical interests are seriously involved.
This, however, is a very questionable view. Difficult as it might be,
man *is* capable of objectivity in scholarship. This is due to the fact that
he is not just an animal, but also something more.

It should also be clear that *the more* one takes a stand on Communism,
the more one should be interested in knowing it. But to know means to
know the object as it is – objectively and impartially. Consequently,
the stand taken should not interfere with the will for objectivity – on
the contrary, it should be an incentive to it.

And yet the difficulty *is* great. When combined with the other difficulties
discussed above, it is really formidable. A Sovietologist should be always
conscious of it and willing to use the maximum of energy in the avoidance
of wishful thinking, which would deprive his work of its value.

A BIBLIOGRAPHY OF SOVIET PHILOSOPHY

The revivification which brought Soviet philosophy out of its pre-1947 "quiet" period was marked by a very significant increase in both the quantity and quality of Soviet philosophic literature. It would have been only natural that this renaissance be accompanied by, and recorded in, bibliographies which would aid researchers to avoid repetition and duplication of effort. Contrary to all expectations, Soviet philosophers, who form a school which is one of the few in contemporary philosophy which is "scientific" in this respect [1], have failed to produce a bibliography which would reflect the development since the "discussion" of 1947.

This is not to say that bibliographies – and some very well-done ones, at that – do not exist in the Soviet Union. There are, in general, three types of bibliography currently being published in the USSR, and in each type one can find information on works dealing with philosophic questions. They are: (1) an annual bibliography of Soviet bibliography [2]; (2) the annual list of books published in the Soviet Union [3]; (3) special bibliographies [4]. In addition, there are mimeographed lists of works pertaining to specific domains, but these are hand-distributed to a very restricted circle of specialists and cannot, therefore, be classified as research-tools available to any investigator, especially Western.[5]

A glance at each of these types of bibliograpy quickly reveals that they are of little help either to a scholar who is interested in concentrated study of some aspect of Soviet philosophy or to the general philosophical reader whose interests are broader. Thus, both the bibliography of Soviet bibliography and the annual list of books are divided into the traditional sections, and books of philosophic interest may be found under any one of the following rubrics: Marxism-Leninism; The Communist Party of the SU; Social Sciences; Philosophy. Socio-Political Doctrine; History; Economic Sciences. Political Economy; Communist Construction of the USSR; Culture. Education. Science; Atheism. Science and Religion. Religion. Therefore, it would not be impossible – at least, in theory – that one find a book on the subject in which one is interested, merely by going through these

sources. But it is evident that the finding of the book would entail an a-
mount of time disproportionate to any result obtained.

A further deficiency of these sources is that they do not contain the articles
of *"Voprosy filosofii"* and *"Filosofskie nauki"*. In view of the fact that most
of the more significant events in contemporary Soviet philosophical life
have been recorded on the pages of the *"Voprosy filosofii"*, this is indeed a
serious lack. It is true that such special bibliographies as "The History of
Science (Bibliography)" [6] do contain the articles of these journals, but these
have value only for those scholars who are dealing in the restricted domain
covered by the bibliography in question – e.g. the last-quoted book would
be a fine source for those dealing with Soviet philosophy of science even
though, again, the entries are scattered in a rather *a priori* distribution.

Since 1952 the editors of the *"Voprosy filosofii"* (VF) have provided a list of
each year's production in the last issue of the year [7], but this leaves 1947 to
1951 unaccounted for and does not take books into account. We do find
occasional book-lists in the *"Voprosy"* but these are of value only as materials for constructing an eventual bibliography.

Thus, all in all, Soviet coverage of contemporary Soviet philosophic
literature has been, to say the least, fragmentary up to now.

It became obvious that if Western researchers were to profitably embark on
investigations of Soviet thought in general and of contemporary Soviet
philosophy in particular, they would need a guide to the literature, and this
guide would have to be more complete and more efficiently organized than
are the Soviet sources. For, in contradistinction to the "quiet" period when
Soviet philosophical production was almost entirely made up of boring and
repetitive quotations from the so-called "classics", the present period
gives signs of genuine philosophical discussion, of the formation of what
might be called "schools" within Dialectical Materialism [8], and of a
tendency to honour, but not slavishly imitate, the "classics" [9]. We find discussions of questions in such domains as ontology, logic, ethics, etc., which
are of definite interest even to the Western philosopher who deals in these
subjects (and who very often has the *a priori* judgement that *nothing* good
can come out of the SU). Therefore, we might say that the need for such a
bibliography was felt first and foremost by those researchers who work
directly in the domain of contemporary Soviet thought, but that the general
philosophical public would profit from having it at hand.

A second circumstance which made the production of such a bibliography necessary was the veritable mountain of Soviet philosophic literature which has appeared since 1947. The *"Voprosy filosofii"* alone, with some 1,000 articles by almost 800 authors between 1947 and 1956, makes up a little library which by Western standards would amount to 50 volumes of 500 pages each. And, whereas there were only 23 philosophic works of 100 pages or more published in 1947, we find some 67 in 1956, with a total of about 500 for the period 1947-1956. Finally, since 1958 a new journal, *"Filosofskie nauki"* (FN), has been added. Scientific selection from this mass of material demanded some type of research-tool which would enable the scholar to find what he needed with speed and accuracy.

Finally, there was a much more pressing reason for producing this bibliography. Very early in the course of the researches undertaken by members of the Institute of East-European Studies in Fribourg (Switzerland) – the summaries of which form the subject-matter of the present volume – it appeared that some type of bibliography which would facilitate the location and use of pertinent Soviet philosophic literature, was an absolute necessity. Since no such work was available and since, to all appearances, it did not seem that the Soviets themselves were about to do anything in this line, the only solution was for the Institute to provide itself with this necessary tool of research. The result was the two-volume "Bibliography of Soviet Philosophy" [10].

Because this bibliography was urgently needed, and because it was intended primarily for the investigator who is working directly in Soviet philosophy and from Russian sources, no effort was made to provide translations – the subject-index has proved to be of more use than translations would have been.

The first volume includes all the articles of the *"Voprosy filosofii"* from 1947 to 1956, while the second is divided into two main sections: (1) Soviet philosophical books published in the period 1947-1956; (2) Soviet philosophical books, and articles from the *"Voprosy filosofii"* and *"Filosofskie nauki"*, for the period 1957-1958. Both volumes contain a list of books reviewed in the journals listed above; the first volume has a comprehensive subject-index, while the second contains a name-index for both volumes. Each list is an alphabetic ordering of the last names of the authors and each entry is numbered serially so that cross-reference, whether it be in the subject-index, name-index or list of books reviewed, is according to this number and not by page number.

If there is no improvement in the situation of the bibliography of philosophy on the part of the Soviets themselves, the "Bibliography of Soviet Philosophy" will continue to appear every two or three years, since many of the works which are presented in the present volume – for example, the works on Soviet method and on Soviet logic – would have been significantly more difficult and longer in the making without such a basic research-tool as is the "Bibliography".

REFERENCES

1. See J. M. Bocheński: *Der sowjetrussische dialektische Materialismus* (Diamat). Aufl. 3. Bern. 1960 (English edition in preparation).
2. *Bibliografija Sovetskoj bibliografii*. Izd. Vsesojuznoj Knižnaja palaty. Moskva (yearly).
3. *Ežegodnik knigi SSSR*. Izd. Vsesojuznoj Knižnaja palaty. Moskva (yearly).
4. e.g. *Istorija estestvoznanija (Bibliografičeskij ukazatel') 1948-1950*. AN SSSR. Moskva. 1955. Aseeva, N.V.: *Kompleksnaja mexanizacija i avtomatizacija – kryl'ja semiletki (Obzor literatury)*. Leningrad. 1960. *Bibliografičeskij ukazatel' literatury po torfy*. Moskva. 1960. Piskunov, A. I.: *Sovetskaja istoriko-pedagogičeskaja literatura (Sist. ukazatel')*. Moskva. 1960.
5. For example, on pages 6 and 7 of *"Bibliografija Sovetskoj bibliografii"* for 1956 we find that the section on Dialectical and Historical Materialism contains eight entries: four are vulgarizations, two from journals (one of which is from *"Voprosy filosofii"* see note 7 below), and the other two are mimeographed.
6. *Istorija estestvoznanija (Bibliografičeskij ukazatel') 1948-1950*. Moskva. 1955.
7. For example, *Ukazatel' statej, pomeščennyx v žurnale "Voprosy filosofii" v 1959 godu*. VF 1959, 12, 183–190.
8. Bocheński, J. M.: *Einführung in die sowjetische Philosophie der Gegenwart*. In: Aus Politik und Zeitgeschichte B45/59. p. 608f.
9. *ibid.* p. 604.
10. *Bibliographie der sowjetischen Philosophie*. 1. die "Voprosy filosofii" 1947–1956 (Sovietica. Veröffentlichungen des Ost-Europa Instituts, Univ. Freiburg Schweiz. 1). 2. Bücher 1947–1956. Bücher und Aufsätze 1957–1958 (Sovietica. Veröffentlichungen 2). Dordrecht. 1959.

T. BLAKELEY

METHOD IN SOVIET PHILOSOPHY *

The need for a study of Soviet philosophic method is, perhaps, seen most clearly in the fact that Western observers are unanimous in characterising contemporary Soviet philosophy as "dogmatic", while contemporary Soviet philosophers themselves are just as unanimous in maintaining that theirs is a "scientific" philosophy – indeed, the sole scientific philosophy. In order to solve this dilemma we asked ourselves the following questions: "What method (i.e. procedure) do contemporary Soviet philosophers use in the discussion and development of Dialectical Materialism?" [1]; "To what extent, if any, can this method be called a dogmatic procedure, and to what extent, if any, can it be called scientific?"; "What is the real significance of this method?"; "For what reasons has it been accepted by contemporary Soviet philosophers?".

In one form or another, these very same questions have been posed, and rather extensively discussed, by contemporary Soviet philosophers themselves. In fact, the so-called "Marxist dialectical method" is presented in such works as "The Marxist Dialectical Method" by M. M. Rozental' [2] as the sole scientific method. Closer consideration of the numerous descriptions of this method, in the many works of Rozental' and other contemporary Soviet "methodologists", makes it obvious that what they describe as method is precisely not the method of science as this is conceived in the West – it is a general theory of reality and of the relationship between human thought and reality, i.e. an ontology and epistemology rather than a methodology. The essential characteristics of the "Marxist dialectical method", as described by Soviet philosophers, can be reduced to the following: (1) It is a method; hence it must "reflect" reality and correspond to its object; (2) It is "dialectical"; therefore, it reflects the "objective dialectic" which is "the most general laws of nature, society and human thought"; (3) Its origins, its applications and its very formulation are oriented toward the natural sciences; (4) It is a "tool" and "guide" for the

* Blakeley, T.: *Soviet Scholasticism* (Sovietica Monographs). Dordrecht (in print).

"understanding and transformation of reality"; (5) It is "Marxist"; therefore, it is "revolutionary-critical" and "party-minded". Even those elements of genuine methodology (as we understand it) which are offered by these thinkers on the margin, so to speak, of their ontological, epistemological and psychological considerations are prominent because of their very scarcity and simplicity. Therefore, the Soviet theory of the "Marxist dialectical method" gives us no satisfactory answer to the question posed on the nature of the method used by contemporary Soviet philosophers.

Having examined the methodological *theory* of contemporary Soviet philosophy and found it lacking, we turn to an examination of the *practice* of contemporary Soviet philosophers in their development of Dialectical Materialism. The materials used in this research include some 1800 items – books like G.E. Glezerman's "Base and Superstructure in Soviet Society"[3], G. F. Aleksandrov's "Dialectical Materialism"[4], I. D. Pancxava's work of the same name[5]; articles from the *"Voprosy filosofii"*, *"Filosofskie nauki"*, *"Kommunist"*, etc.; articles from such encyclopedias and lexica as the "Large Soviet Encyclopedia". This material by no means represents the totality of contemporary Soviet philosophic production from 1947 to 1959 inclusive, but it does offer a cross-section of the work being done by Soviet philosophers today. Examined from the point of view of method – i.e. paying attention not to what was said but to how what was said was justified – it revealed that the basic procedure employed by contemporary Soviet philosophers is "dogmatic", thus corroborating the opinion of Western observers, but that it is also characterized by certain "scientific" traits such as one would expect to find principally in the so-called empirical sciences.

Briefly stated, contemporary Soviet philosophy is "dogmatic" because the so-called "classics of Marxism-Leninism" are the point of departure and and the "court of last resort" in all philosophic discussions in the Soviet Union; it is "scientific" because – as Soviet philosophers never tire of repeating – it is "verified" by every advance of scientific knowledge and by the progress of "socialist construction in the USSR and the peoples' democracies".

An examination of what Soviet theoreticians, from Stalin and Khrushchov to the most insignificant of contemporary Soviet propagandists, have to *say* about the so-called "classics" shows that there is a doctrine, called

"Marxism-Leninism", which is the official doctrine of the Communist Party of the Soviet Union; that "Marxism-Leninism" is the teaching of the "classics", i.e. "K. Marx, F. Engels and V.I. Lenin" [6]; that the doctrine of the "classics", "Marxism-Leninism", is held to be the last word in all fields of knowledge and is, as to essentials, not to be questioned.

Turning to an analysis of what contemporary Soviet philosophers *do*, we find that their writings can be divided roughly into two groups, exegetic commentaries on the works of the "classics of Marxist-Leninist philosophy", and more independent treatises on philosophic questions. Even though we can notice a marked evolution toward more independent speculations, the majority of contemporary Soviet philosophic publications are no more nor less than commentaries on the writings of the "classics". But the methodologically most significant characteristic of contemporary Soviet philosophic procedure is the fact that the contemporary Soviet philosopher proceeds from a certain set of propositions, which are called "principles of Marxism-Leninism" and are statements of the "classics", by *deduction* to conclusions which are admitted into the system only if they can be shown not to contradict the statements of these same "classics". The basic assumptions on which the theoretical constructs of Soviet philosophers depend as on the axioms of a deductive system are: the primacy of being over thought; the materiality of the objective world; the dialectical character of reality; and the "reflection" theory of knowledge. These four propositions are accepted as axioms, i.e. without critical examination, and are at the basis of all subsequent Soviet theorizing. What is more, the basic pattern of the argumentation is rigorously the same whether the author in question be dealing with matter, motion, space and time, the "dialectic", logic (formal or "dialectical"), theory of knowledge, categories or "the basic question of all philosophy": the "problem" is posed by a "classic" and a deduction is made, the conclusion of which is "confirmed" by a "classic". Therefore, in so far as the basic argumentation of contemporary Soviet philosophy is a deduction from principles which are accepted, without critical examination, from an authority which lies outside the domain of philosophy, it can be termed "dogmatic".

But contemporary Soviet philosophers hold that the propositions of "Marxism-Leninism" are established both by the course of history, i.e. by social events, and by all of the advances of the natural sciences. They contend, to put it rather bluntly, that there is nothing which happens which is not a confirmation of the "theory of Marxism-Leninism". The authors of the *"Osnovy marksistskoj filosofii"* [7] – the official exposition of contemporary Soviet philosophy – sum up this point of view, which is that of each and every contemporary Soviet philosopher, when they say: "The entire course of world history for the last century irrefutably proves the truthfulness of the principles of Marxism-Leninism and of the laws revealed by it. Just as the Great October Socialist Revolution and the victory of socialism in the USSR, the victory of the socialist revolution in China and a string of other countries, was the triumph and the confirmation of the truth of the laws of Historical Materialism, so the striking discoveries of contemporary science are the triumph and confirmation of the truthfulness of Dialectical Materialism." [8]

Here we touch on the characteristic of contemporary Soviet philosophic procedure which serves most to distinguish it from the procedures found in all other currents of contemporary philosophy [9]; that characteristic is the simultaneous use of two distinct and seemingly mutually exclusive methods of argumentation – appeal to extra-philosophic authority or *recourse to the "classics"* and "veri..cation" or *recourse to "experience"*. Obviously, this brings up the venerable question as to whether or not one and the same person can know and believe the same proposition at the same time. Philosophers who answer in the negative are generally classed as "rationalists" or "intellectualists", while those who answer in the affirmative are often classed as "irrationalists".

The anomaly tends to disappear when we conceive, as a *working hypothesis*, the procedure used by contemporary Soviet philosophers as having a basically hypothetico-deductive structure wherein the stage of hypothesis-formation is considered as having been already completed by the so-called "classics of Marxism-Leninism" and the deductive stage with its consequent verification is that now being effected by the "workers on the ideological front".

The first, or hypothesis-formation stage, which is considered as having been accomplished by the so-called "classics of Marxist-Leninist philosophy", can be represented as follows: the "classics of Marxism-Leninism", i.e. Marx, Engels and Lenin, took statements about facts (in the present instance, facts of 19th century science, sociology and history of philosophy for Marx and Engels; facts of the early 20th for Lenin) and constructed hypotheses, i.e. proposed general theories which would explain the totality or, at least, a major portion of these facts. It is important to note here that the question of whether or not the "classics" thought or said that they were constructing hypotheses, or even of whether or not they actually did construct hypotheses and did not lay down dogmata, is entirely irrelevant to the present discussion. The fact is that contemporary Soviet philosophers do conceive "Marxist-Leninist philosophy" as marked by at least two ear-marks of the so-called positive or empirical sciences – that of "hypothesis-projection" or generalization on the basis of facts, and that of making, in function of these hypotheses or generalizations, certain types of "predictions" which are to be proved or disproved in some sort of process of verification. Since contemporary Soviet philosophers do attribute these two characteristics, which we consider to be typical of the natural sciences and to methodologically imply a hypothetico-deductive procedure, to "Marxism-Leninism", and since they consider this same "Marxism-Leninism" to be the "doctrine of the classics of Marxism-Leninism", then is seems that contemporary Soviet philosophers conceive the work of the "classics" in a "hypothetico-deductive" sense.

The second stage, that of deduction and verification, is central to our consideration of contemporary Soviet philosophic procedure because it is here that we see what makes this procedure unusual, if not unique, in the annals of recent philosophy. The description of what "Soviet method" is requires a consideration of the following elements: those factors, here called *meta-dogmata*,[10] which are responsible for the fact that the pronouncements of the "classics" are accepted by contemporary Soviet philosophers as "dogma"; "meta-dogmata", viz. the *proletarian redemption* of mankind and the *Communist destiny* of humanity, which will help explain not only why the statements of the "classics" are accepted as "dogma" in contemporary Soviet philosophy but also why the Communist Party of the Soviet Union is the accepted authority in all ideological matters; finally, in the light of the information presented on the "meta-dogmata", certain characteristics of contemporary Soviet thought, such as its claim to be the sole valid philosophical system and its out-of-hand and complete rejection of everything which differs from the "Marxist-Leninist line of the Party", phenomena which we call *exclusion of negative cases*, will be made more easily understandable.

Distinguishing three levels of discourse in contemporary Soviet philosophy, we find that the dogmata are the statements of fact dealing with the nature of matter, motion, the "dialectic", categories, etc; the first-level meta-dogmata are propositions dealing with the authority of the Party, especially in ideological matters; the second-level meta-dogmata or meta-dogmata in the full sense of the term are the "proletarian redemption" and "Communist destiny". If we view the situation for a moment from the standpoint of a contemporary Soviet philosopher, we see that the process runs, logically and not necessarily chronologically, somewhat as follows. By a first "act of faith" he accepts the second-level meta-dogmata, i.e. the "proletarian redemption" and "Communist destiny". A second "act of faith", consequent on the first puts him in the situation of admitting the authority of the Party in ideological matters. This puts him in a position to develop and discuss "Marxism-Leninism" without being in any danger of being confused by the fact that the propositions with which he deals are "accepted on faith" and "verified" at one and the same time and in one and the same respect.

"Proletarian redemption" is a term which stands for a complex proposition in which is expressed one of the fundamental "beliefs" of contemporary Soviet philosophers – it is made up of two distinct propositions; the first designates the "proletariat" as having a special destiny, as being charged by history with a special mission; the second justifies the first on the grounds that the interests of the "proletariat" coincide with the interests of mankind, with the objective course of history. A close examination of these propositions shows that they each contain an element which is not rational, i.e. not able to be established by arguments of reason as distinguished from acts of faith, for "proletariat" is taken as identical with "mankind" in a sort of mystical, fideistic insight into the future when all will be "Communist".

The meta-dogma which we call "Communist destiny" can be expressed in the simple proposition: "the destiny of mankind lies in the downfall of capitalism and the full triumph of Communism". It takes no profound analysis to show that this proposition states as certain a future, contingent, event. We see, then, that these basic propositions of the Communist "Weltanschauung", if accepted, are not accepted on the basis of scientific confirmation; rather more, they are so formulated in the some 200 texts which we presented in evidence, that they cannot admit of rational justification. The *dogmatism* of contemporary Soviet philosophy is the result of an *ideological commitment* on the part of the contemporary Soviet philosopher. Because this commitment is an "act of faith", it is absolute, it is complete; it is a *total* commitment. By accepting the "proletarian redemption" and the "Communist destiny" dogmatically, i.e. on non-rational grounds, the contemporary Soviet philosopher commits himself to the acceptance of whatever consequences, however irrational, may be entailed by these meta-dogmata. He is, so to speak, *engaged;* engaged in the acceptance of the so-called "proletarian philosophy of Marx, Engels, Lenin". This is, indeed, the touchstone of Soviet dogmatism. The very acceptance of the authority of the so-called "classics of Marxism-Leninism" is to be seen only in the context of this total ideological commitment, for belief in the certitude of the meta-dogmata is belief in the certitude of the central theses of the so-called "classics" and, since the other theses of "Marxism-Leninism" are considered as subsidiary or subordinate to these central theses, a belief in the certitude of the subsidiary theses is concomitant with belief in the certitude of these two central theses, hence acceptance of the authority of their authors.

In the light of this analysis of Soviet dogmatism we are able to offer an explanation for the simultaneous presence of a type of *verification* in contemporary Soviet philosophy. We have seen that belief in the certainty of the meta-dogmata *is* belief in the pronouncements of the "classics" and *entails* belief in the "principles of Marxist-Leninist philosophy". But, as a matter of fact, it seems that all of the basic principles of "Marxism-Leninism" (namely, the primacy of being over thought, the materiality of the objective world, the "dialectical" character of reality, the "reflective" nature of knowledge) are, at least in principle, verifiable, i.e. could be shown to be true or false, more or less probable. And we could, then, represent contemporary Soviet philosophy as a dogmatic system which is imperfectly formed, certain of the principles of which can be *believed and rationally justified.* However, a closer look at the Soviet "verification" shows that the "principles of Marxism-Leninism" are "demonstrated" *en bloc* by the "accomplishments of the working class" and by "socialist construction". In other words, the principles of "Marxism-Leninism" are "established" by means of *meta-dogmatic verification.* This very obviously means that the "verification" found in contemporary Soviet philosophy is not a verification at all in the sense in which this term is understood in Western science or philosophy.

Thus, our explanation of the *dogmatism and verification* of contemporary

Soviet philosophic procedure, in terms of the meta-dogmata, can be reduced to the following essentials: The meta-dogmata are the "proletarian redemption" and the "Communist destiny". The act of faith by which the contemporary Soviet philosopher accepts the meta-dogmata elicits simultaneously from him an acceptance of the authority of the "classics". All other statements which are part of "Marxist-Leninist philosophy" are accepted dogmatically, that is to say, in function of this primordial belief or act of faith. The so-called "verification" of contemporary Soviet philosophy is fundamentally the same mode of argumentation, i.e. meta-dogmatically controlled, but expressed in a somewhat more scientific form. Finally, it should be stressed that the acceptance of the meta-dogmata, the ideological commitment, by the contemporary Soviet philosopher is to a great extent a matter of emotion and not of reason. This, it seems, has its origin in the emotional voluntarism of the "classics". Marx's view of the future society was definitely clouded by what he thought should be – his hopes for the future were a reaction to the miseries he saw. Our best evidence as to the utopian character of Marx's dreams is the frequent revisions they have undergone at the hands of his Soviet followers. In any case, it is such an emotional desire or need which contemporary Soviet philosophers fill when they accept the meta-dogmata.

As was pointed out above, the present explanation of contemporary Soviet philosophic procedure is in the nature of a working hypothesis. As such, its sole value resides in its aptness to give us an insight into the salient characteristics of that which is being studied. As a matter of fact, our exposition of "Soviet method" in terms of dogma, meta-dogmata and meta-dogmatic verification gives us the possibility of explaining two striking peculiarities of current Soviet thought. First, an examination of the abundant, relevant texts from *"Voprosy filosofii"*, *"Kommunist"*, etc., shows that the contemporary Soviet philosopher accepts the authority of the Party in philosophy because he sees the Party as identified with the "proletariat" and as, therefore, sharing in the "proletarian redemption"; further, believing the "Communist destiny" of mankind to be a certainty, he sees the authority of the Party in philosophy justified by the Party's function as "guide toward Communism". Second, we are able to offer an explanation of that phenomenon which seems to be typical of contemporary Soviet philosophy and of no other and which we call the *exclusion of negative cases*, i.e. an attitude which holds that "Marxism-Leninism" is correct and

24

that all other systems of thought are wrong. The contemporary Soviet philosopher proceeds somewhat as follows: from the axioms of "Marxist-Leninist philosophy", which he treats as if they were hypotheses set up by the "classics", he deduces conclusions, to the "verification" of which he proceeds by observation, usually phenomenal. Up to this point the analogy with the procedure of the scientist is quite close. If the inference he had made corresponds to subsequent observations, then he speaks of "irrefutable proof of the veracity of Marxism-Leninism"; if, on the contrary, the inference is not borne out by further observations, then the observations or "facts" are revised or rejected.[11] Thus, contemporary Soviet philosophers hold "Marxism-Leninism" to be the only valid philosophy and reject all others as erroneous. Or, to put it in terms with which we are by now familiar, the contemporary Soviet philosopher by *meta-dogmatic verification* accepts all events and theories which are defined by the Party as genuine, that is, in line with the "historical mission of the proletariat" and the "Communist destiny of mankind", as "proofs" of the principles of "Marxism-Leninism", and rejects (as "idealist") or revises all events and theories which do not conform or are contrary to these three conditions.

As in any attempt to outline the essentials of a process, our explanation simplifies a procedure which is in reality very complex. But it seems that it contains all the elements basic to an investigation and clarification of the other characteristics which are peculiar to contemporary Soviet philosophy. Thus, "party-mindedness" (*partijnost'*) is a consequence, not the cause, of the *dogmatic attitude* of contemporary Soviet philosophers. And the *exegetic character* of a large part of contemporary Soviet philosophic literature is seen to be a natural consequence of the *meta-dogmatic* assumptions which can exist only in function of an authority. Finally, the *unity of theory and practice* which is a dominant theme of contemporary Soviet philosophy is an involuntary exteriorization of the *unity of dogmatism and empirical verification.*

In conclusion, we might point out that there is a striking parallel between contemporary Soviet philosophy and the movement in medieval philosophy known as Scholasticism. To the superficial observer no two systems could be farther apart than the theologically oriented thought of the schoolmen and the openly atheistic dogmatism of 20th century Marxism-

Leninism. A second look shows that both are, with the necessary qualifications, mainly deductive, ideologically oriented, traditional (i.e. employing an "argument from authority"); more importantly, both are realist in the sense that they are actively engaged in the vital problems of their times. But, looking deeper, we see that these parallels are vitiated by a difference which is, to say the least, essential. For Scholastic philosophy the problem of the relationship of faith and knowledge was primordial – and the solution of this question provoked some of the most magnificent analyses of human belief and human knowledge which are known to us. For the Scholastic philosopher, beyond the limits of human reason, there lay a vast plain to be explored with the eyes of faith. The Scholastic, as a theologian, was inspired by a *supernatural faith*, a faith *in a divine revelation* the certainty of which depends on a *God who revealed*. This being the case, the Scholastic, as a philosopher, could push his researches to the limit, i.e. to full possibilities of his intellectual resources, with the assurance that, if his results seemed to be at variance with what was revealed, he would know that his philosophic researches have to be re-examined since the certitude given to revealed truth by the revealing God is an absolute. The case of the contemporary Soviet philosopher is not at all the same. If we may use the same terms as in the case of the Scholastic, we would say that the contemporary Soviet philosopher, as a "theologian" (hence, when speaking *metadogmatically*), is inspired by a *natural faith* in a *human revelation* the certainty of which is purely and simply a derivation of the *subjective aspirations of the individual*. As immediate consequence, the contemporary Soviet philosopher, as philosopher, finds his researches limited not by the possibilities of his intellectual resources but by the *danger of refutation* which is *necessarily present to a human revelation* (which is no revelation, in the final analysis) and which *constantly threatens a natural faith* (which is, in the end, not a faith but a camouflaged refusal to think).

There is what we might call a fundamental *lack of intellectual honesty* on the part of contemporary Soviet philosophers. More precisely, the very bases of contemporary Soviet philosophic activity are put in question by the failure (or refusal or inability?) of contemporary Soviet philosophers to see the problem of faith and knowledge which is implicit in a great part of their intellectual activity. By denying that they are believers, contemporary Soviet philosophers put themselves in an untenable position, *an irrational position*. It seems clear that before contemporary Soviet philosophy can take a place as a system *of thought*, its exponents must face the problem of faith and knowledge honestly and find a solution which will allow Soviet philosophers, when philosophizing, to be free from the trammels of a restrictive dogmatism.

REFERENCES

1. We restrict our consideration to Dialectical Materialism since, according to current Soviet doctrine, Historical Materialism is Diamat as found in society. See *Osnovy Marksistskoj filosofii.* Moskva. 1958. (p. 349f.)
2. M. M. Rozental' is currently the leading Soviet methodologist. Among his works in this domain: *Marksistskij dialektičeskij metod.* Moskva. 1947. *Voprosy dialektiki v "Kapitale" Marksa.* Moskva. 1955. *Veliki vklad v marksistskuju teoriju poznanija.* VF 1959, 5, 18–32.
3. Glezerman, G. E.: *Bazis i nadstrojka v Sovetskom obščestve.* Moskva. 1954.
4. Aleksandrov, G. F.: *Dialektičeskij materializm.* Moskva. 1953.
5. Pancxava, I. D.: *Dialektičeskij materializm.* Moskva. 1958.
6. During his lifetime, I. V. Stalin occupied the privileged position of "classic" and "official interpreter of the 'classics'". Since the 20th Party Congress he has ceased to figure in the litany of the "classics". Nevertheless, as recently as October 1959, his "Marxism and the National Question" figures under the rubric "Works of the Classics of Marxism" in Voprosy's list of "New Books for Philosophy and Sociology" (see VF 1959, 10, 182).
7. *Osnovy marksistskoj filosofii.* (editor) F. V. Konstantinov. Moskva. 1958. Henceforward: Osnovy.
8. See Osnovy p. 3.
9. See J. M. Bocheński: *Contemporary European Philosophy.* Berkeley and Los Angeles. 1956.
10. By "dogma" we mean a proposition which is accepted on the basis of an extra-philosophic authority, in function of a sort of faith. By "meta-dogma" we mean a proposition which is not only itself a dogma but also is the reason why the dogmata of a given system are accepted on faith. It should be noticed that a sufficiently developed dogmatic system generally has at least three classes of propositions, we might say three levels of discourse. There are the dogmata properly so-called, which state a fact and no more. Then there are what might be called the "first-level meta-dogmata", which are propositions which deal with the competence of an authority to prescribe belief in the dogmata. Finally, there are propositions which could be called "second-level meta-dogmata" or, more precisely, meta-dogmata in the full sense of the term.
11. The rejection of the Mendel-Morgan theory of "genes" and of Einstein's theory of relativity are only the more famous cases of denial of scientifically fruitful hypotheses on purely ideological grounds. In reference to the theory of relativity, see S. Müller-Markus: *Einstein und die Sowjetphilosophie. Krisis einer Lehre.* I (Sovietica Abhandlungen 1). Dordrecht. 1960 and the summary thereof in the present volume.

J. M. BOCHEŃSKI

SOVIET LOGIC

The scope of this paper is the presentation of a survey of the development of recent Soviet logic and the main topics therein discussed. By "recent" is meant the period since 1947, and "logic" means *general* logic, i.e. the group of disciplines made up of formal logic, logical semiotics, the methodology of science and the study of such problems as can be conveniently classified as belonging to the philosophy of logic [1].

Little has been written in the West on this subject. There is a short but substantial treatment of the 1950/51 discussion in the classical work of Fr. Wetter [2]; Dr. Dahm devoted a very erudite paper to the development of formal logic [3]; the main publications belonging to the field of formal logic were masterfully reviewed in the "Journal of Symbolic Logic" by Prof. G. Kline,[4] the most competent scholar in the field; Mr. G. Küng has a bibliography of Soviet symbolic logic [5] now in print; and, lastly, Prof. N. Lobkowicz published a valuable collection of texts concerning the great discussion on contradictions (1958) [6]. In Russian, there is also a study by Prof. Philipov [7] which, unfortunately, was not available to the present writer.

Yet the subject is not without interest. Not only is there in the Soviet Union an active school of formal logicians in the departments of mathematics, but also the developments in other sections of general logic offer some striking peculiarities which seem to be relevant to the systematic and historical problems connected with logic. The general impression one receives from the study of our field is that Soviet logic speedily developed during the past twelve years or so under circumstances which brought to the fore some problems which are seldom if ever treated in the West, while some questions which are disputed there were here (in the SU) treated in a somewhat different way.

The history of Soviet philosophy is usually divided into three periods: the first period of discussions (up to January 1931); the "dead" period (1931 to June 1947); and the contemporary period of discussions [8]. So far as logic is concerned, the last period (with which we are dealing here) begins somewhat earlier, in November 1946. At that time the Central Committee of the CPSU prescribed by decree the introduction of courses on logic and psychology in Soviet schools [9]. Immediately a number of logical textbooks were published [10]. One of them – that by M. S. Strogovič – seems to have appeared even before the decree, i.e. in 1946 [11]. They were all textbooks of the "classical" type, similar to those published in the West around 1900. A period of severe attacks on the authors – above all on Asmus – followed. On 23 March 1948 the Minister for Higher Education, Kaftanov, condemn-ed Asmus' textbook as containing "formal and apolitical" logic [12]. Several "conferences" of logicians were held [13]. Most of the texts published seem to have been severely criticized (VF 50, 2, 209). During these discussions, several important problems were posed and discussed, such as the question of the scientific (apolitical and neutral) character of logic and that of the existence of two or only one logic.

The situation changed rather radically in June 1950 when Stalin published his *ukaz* on language and linguistics [14]. This affirmed that language is not a class-bound phenomenon. Since language, is, according to the "classics", the "body of thought", the same could now be said about thought and, consequently, about logic. A vast discussion was organized by the editors of the *"Voprosy filosofii"* [15]. This discussion marks the beginning of a speedy development of Soviet logic. In 1955/56 another, more restricted, discussion took place between Rozental' [16] and the editors of the VF,[17] on one side, and two leading formal logicians, Bakradze [18] and Kondakov [19], on the other.

In September 1956 a seminar for logic was opened in the Institute of Philosophy of the Academy of Sciences of the USSR. Two years later, in April 1958, an important discussion on contradictions was held in the same institute [20]. A bumper-crop of new textbooks [21] and, also, of more scientific books and papers was forthcoming [22]. At the present time, Soviet logic seems to be in full development and the publications of Soviet logicians and philosophers of logic have already attained, at least in some cases, a good scientific level.

FORMAL LOGIC

Even during the "dead" period, formal logic was cultivated by the mathematicians. There was a solid tradition of studies in symbolic logic in Russia, which began with Poreckij, who published his first paper in 1881 [23]. A. N. Kolmogorov, an intuitionist whose work is appreciated by logicians, started publishing in 1924 [24]. But, until 1947, the Russians had no textbook of mathematical logic. Then that of Hilbert-Ackerman was published [25] and a year later the "Introduction" of Tarski appeared in Russian translation – thanks to Prof. Janovskaja [26]. In 1957, Kleene's "Introduction to Metamathematics" was also translated [27]. The first original Soviet textbook of mathematical logic is that of Novikov, published only in 1959 [28]. Alongside these books, a number of research papers was published. They are quoted in the monumental "Mathematics in the SU During 40 Years" [29], and ably described by Prof. Janovskaja in the same volume [30]. A fuller bibliography of Soviet formal logic has been prepared by Mr. G. Küng [31]. A special mention should be made of the study of technical applications of formal logic [32]. While this was studied primarily by mathematicians, we find, since 1955, a relatively great interest in it among philosophers [33]. A characteristic fact is that some purely technical papers on cybernetics were included in the above-mentioned volume *"Logičeskie Issledovanija"*, edited by the *Institute of Philosophy* of the Academy of Sciences [34]. The classical work of N. Wiener [35] and the book of Ashby [36] have been translated into Russian. We also know of at least one original, technical Soviet work on cybernetics [37] and of one work, rather popular in nature, published in Kiev [38].

However, we have to do in the Soviet Union, as in many other countries, with *two* coexisting sorts of logic. While the mathematicians are developing modern, symbolic logic, the philosophers go on publishing books and research papers of the "classical" type. At the beginning, the distinction in the SU was as clear-cut as in any existentialist Western university [39]. Now, this distinction is tending to disappear. The philosophers are now more and more interested in mathematical logic. Thus, already in 1955, the collective volume published by the Institute of *Philosophy* [40] contained articles belonging at least marginally to mathematical logic. And a similar volume which appeared in 1959 [41] contains studies which belong strictly to this field. Moreover, at the University of Moscow concrete proposals were made for a very extensive program of teaching in mathematical logic and connected disciplines (methodology, semantics, history of logic) [42].

This does not mean, however, that the textbooks used in the departments of philosophy of the Soviet universities and in the lower schools would be in any way similar to those of Prof. Copi or that of the present writer. They are, as far as we know, all of the old, "classical" type – syllogistics, the "four fundamental laws of thought" (the fourth being that of sufficient reason), sophistics and some considerations about induction, mostly taken from John Stuart Mill[43]. Considerable opposition to mathematical logic is still alive among philosophers [44].

On the whole, the situation of formal logic in the SU may be characterized as follows. There is an active school of mathematical logicians of respectable standing; there is some interest in scientific logic among philosophers; but the teaching is mostly still at the pre-Boolean level. However, if we compare the state of affairs in the SU with that in most countries of Western Europe, it seems that there is more good formal logic in the former than in the latter.

METHODOLOGY

There has been in the Soviet Union up to now very little methodology of science, as it is understood in the West. It is true that a number of things have been written about the so-called "dialectical" method, but this seems to be no method at all, in the above meaning of the word [45]. Some writers have dedicated a few papers to such problems as analysis and synthesis[46]. Also, here and there, papers on the role of hypotheses, etc., are appearing [47]. But the present writer does not know of a single significant contribution by Soviet logicians to this science.

SEMANTICS

There is also very little work done in scientific semantics. One reason seems to be the violent repudiation of the supposed "idealism" of the founders of this science, A. Tarski and R. Carnap. The former especially is continuously the target of vicious attacks, and even Prof. Janovskaja has been attacked for having translated his "Introduction" [48]. It must be remarked that the omission of this book (in Russian translation) from Novikov's preface [49] belongs to the most curious facts in recent Soviet logic – it shows how much Soviet logicians are still under the control of ideology.

Yet the very fact that semantics is included in the program mentioned above [42] and the existence of a few papers on semantic problems, shows that some interest in this science does exist.

32

PHILOSOPHY OF LOGIC

In direct contrast, it seems that Soviet logicians did contribute – and even quite seriously – to the philosophy of logic. No other country is known in which so many problems of this displine have been so much discussed as in the Soviet Union and, while many things written are valueless, some others seem to contain interesting ideas.

These writings are difficultly understood by a Western logician because many problems which are examined by him under separate titles tend to be confounded under the common denomination "logic and dialectic". If, however, we consider the arguments closely, it is easy to see that the discussions are very often not about the pseudo-problem of a supposed "dialectical" logic (there is, obviously, no such thing), but about several real and important difficulties. These may be provisionally classified as follows:

(1) Is there a purely formal logic or must every logic be considered as "material", i.e. bound to a subject matter?

(2) Taking for granted that there is a purely formal logic, is this *all* of logic or must it be supplemented by other logical disciplines?

(3) Is methodology a part of logic (i.e. depends upon and uses the principles of formal logic) or must it be considered as a "philosophic" science which might be cultivated independently of formal logic?

(4) What is the relation of logical laws to those of reality? Can we, for example, say that the principle of contradiction is a valid logical law but does not apply to reality?

(5) What is the relationship of logical laws and entities to the flux of ever-changing events?

(6) Is logic necessarily bound up with an epistemology and, therefore, must be divided according to the several epistemological standpoints (e.g. the realist and the idealist), or is it an epistemologically neutral science?

(7) The problem of universals: are there, in any meaning of the word, universals *in re*?

(8) Is logic a philosophical discipline or does it belong rather to mathematics? If the former, can mathematical logic be considered to be a logic at all?

It is the belief of the present writer that these problems, some of which were elaborated in hard struggle by Soviet logicians,[50] have never been sufficiently studied, from the modern point of view, by any school of Western logicians. Moreover, not even the efforts of Soviet logicians are really known; we do not have a single study on any of the above problems which were so much discussed by them.

As we do not yet have studies on these subjects, it is not possible to describe with precision the attitudes taken by Soviet logicians. Yet a general orientation may be ventured. Soviet thinkers seem to fall into three classes. First, there are those who really do not know logic, but are still talking about it – a phenomenon well known also in the West. One instance of such an attitude is offered by the paper published in 1951 by Majstrov and Tugarinov [51]. Another group is composed of philosophers who know their logic but try to interpret it in the framework of Hegelian categories. The most conspicuous example of this is A.D. Aleksandrov, whose contribution to the 1950/51 discussion is certainly a very able effort to supply mathematical logic with a Hegelian basis [52]. These thinkers would, of course, insist on the limitations of formal logic, pretend that reality is governed by quite different laws than those it contains, assert the philosophic and material character of full logic, and so on. Finally, there is an outspoken Aristotelian trend, represented above all by Bakradze and Kondakov as well as by a group of younger men like those who argued for the real applicability of the principle of contradiction in 1958 [53]. For them, formal logic is the *only* logic in the strict sense of the word. There is no other "fuller" and "deeper" logic. Of course, they will admit the existence of a methodology and of a philosophy of logic – they are developing their own on rather strictly Aristotelian lines – but all these disciplines are based on logic which is, for them, an autonomous discipline [54].

It seems that these discussions, which still await closer examination, are important not only because they might bring some new insights in this difficult field, but also for the understanding of what is happening in Soviet philosophy. The logical discussions do exemplify, in a most striking manner, the old truth that Dialectical Materialism is composed of two opposed factors, the so-called "dialectic", which is Hegelian, and the so-called "materialism, "which is, basically, nothing else but an Aristotelian view of reality. Whenever real effort is made to think Dialectical Materialism through, Soviet thinkers fall apart and follow either the first or the second line.

HISTORY OF LOGIC

There is also, in the Soviet Union, some attention paid to the history of logic. Ancient formal logic has been studied – in a competent way – by A.S. Axmanov [55]. The "Analytics" [56] of Aristotle were newly translated in 1952. From a report by Zinov'ev [57] and a paper of Stjažkin [58] we learn that research work has been done in medieval logic. Even if some of the results quoted are of no revolutionary import, still they are interesting. Much attention has been devoted to Russian logic of the period of decadence. We have in that field a bibliography by Primakovskij [59], an edition of texts by Tavanec, and a study on Georgian logic by Kalandaršvili [60]. An interesting study of the main developments in philosophy of logic in modern times – a unique achievement as far as we know – is due to the pen of Asmus [61]. The program of logical studies already mentioned provided for a large section concerned with the history of logic. This is very extensive indeed – for example, it mentions a special course on the Polish logical school.

On the whole, the history of logic is still in its beginnings in the SU but seems to be developing satisfactorily.

GENERAL APPRECIATION

A few details, referred to above in a sketchy way, justify the general conclusion that not only mathematical logic but also the philosophy of logic and some other relevant disciplines have developed considerably since 1947. It is, perhaps, the field in which the qualitative progress of Soviet thought is the most evident. The results achieved are by no means spectacular – yet, on the whole, the Soviet Union seems to have risen to a position which is not very much worse than that of many other important countries.

If one considers the enormous difficulties, due to the barbaric *forma mentis* prevailing in high places in the SU, with which Soviet logicians have had to fight, their achievements must be termed very remarkable. They allow considerable hope for the future.

But even what has already been achieved certainly merits the attention of Western logicians and philosophers. A more adequate study of Soviet logic now seems to be a necessity [62].

REFERENCES

1. For a fuller justification of this terminology, see J. Bocheński: *Formale Logik*. Freiburg i/B. 1956. pp. 3–5.
2. Wetter, G. A.: *Dialectical Materialism*. London. 1958. pp. 523–535.
3. Dahm, H.: *Renaissance der formalen Logik*. In: Ost-Probleme 1957, 8, 254–267.
4. JSL 14, 1949, 243f.; 16, 1951, 46–48; 17, 1952, 124–129; 18, 1953, 83–86 and 271f.; 19, 1954, 149.
5. Küng, G.: *A Bibliography of Soviet Mathematical Logic*. Ms. in the Institute of East-European Studies, University of Fribourg, Switzerland.
6. Lobkowicz, N.: *Das Widerspruchsprinzip in der neueren sowjetischen Philosophie*. Dordrecht. 1959.
7. Philipov, A.: *Logic and Dialectic in the Soviet Union*. New York. 1952.
8. See J. M. Bocheński: *Der sowjetrussische dialektische Materialismus* (Diamat). Bern. 1956. (pp. 35ff.) and *Einführung in die sowjetische Philosophie der Gegenwart*. In: Aus Politik und Zeitgeschichte. B 45/59. Bonn. 1959 (p. 597). On the "dead" period, see also the qualifications by Wetter in *op. cit.* pp. 175–181. In logic perhaps more than elsewhere, it is quite incorrect to speak about a "Stalinist" period; it was Stalin who operated the "liberalization" after having imposed silence.
9. Both Wetter (*op cit.* second German edition p. 544 – corrected in the English edition) and myself (Diamat 1950 p. 133) put that decree erroneously in 1947. The error has been corrected by Dahm in *op cit.* p. 254f. See also BSE ed. 2, vol. 25, p. 336.
10. Such as: Čelpanov (a new – somewhat corrected – edition of a pre-revolution textbook), Strogovič, Asmus and Vinogradov.
11. Strogovič, M. S.: *Logika*. Moskva. 1956. It is interesting to note that this is a textbook destined for the military academy.
12. Osmakov VF 1948, 2, 376.
13. End of June 1948 (Osmakov *loc. cit.*); July 1949 (VF 1951, 6, 144); March 1950 (Osmakov VF 1950, 3, 330).
14. *Marksizm i voprosy jazykoznanija*. Moskva. 1950. (English: Marxism and Problems of Linguistics. Moscow–London. 1954/5.)
15. VF 1950, 2 to 1951, 6. German translations in: *Über formale Logik und Dialektik*. Berlin. 1952. 216 S.
16. VF 1955, 2, 218–224.
17. VF 1955, 3, 158–171; 1956, 2, 229–236.
18. VF 1956, 2, 218–224.
19. VF 1956, 2, 224–238.
20. See Lobkowicz *op. cit.* and his article in this volume.
21. Gorskij, D. P.: *Logika*. Moskva. 1958 is one example.
22. e.g.: *Books:* Alekseev, M. N.: *Dialektika form myšlenija*. Moskva. 1959. *Logičeskie issledovanija*. Moskva. 1959. *Problemy dialektičeskoj logiki*. Moskva. 1959. Reznikov, L. O.: *Ponjatie i slovo*. Leningrad. 1958. *Voprosy logiki*. Leningrad. 1959. *Articles:* Drozdov, A. V.: *O suščnosti i sostave sub'ekta i predikata suždenija*. In: *Voprosy logiki*. Leningrad. 1959 (pp. 28–36). Getmanova, A. D.: *O sootnošenii logiki i matematiki v sistemax tipa Principia Mathematica*. In: *Logičeskie issledovanija*. Moskva. 1959 (pp. 189–217). Kol'man, E.: *Značenie simboličeskoj logiki*. In: *Logičeskie issledovanija*. Moskva. 1959 (pp. 3–19). Zinov'ev, A. A.: *Problema značenij istinnosti v mnogoznačnoj logike*. VF 1959, 3, 131–136.

36

23. Church, A.: *A Bibliography of Symbolic Logic*. In: JSL 1, 1936, p. 136, N. 58.
24. *Ibid.* p. 191, N. 314.
25. Gil'bert, D., Akkerman, V.: *Osnovy teoretičeskoj logiki*. Moskva. 1947.
26. Tarskij, A.: *Vvedenie v logiku i metodologiju deduktivnyx nauk*. Moskva. 1948.
27. Kleene, S.: *Vvedenie v metamatematiku*. Moskva. 1957.
28. Novikov, P. S.: *Elementy matematičeskoj logiki*. Moskva. 1959. The book of Popov, A. I.: *Vvedenie v matematičeskuju logiku* (Leningrad. 1959), was not available to the writer.
29. *Matematika v SSSR za sorok let.* 1959 (2 vols.).
30. Janovskaja, S. A.: *Matematičeskaja logika i osnovnaja matematika*. In: *ibid.* pp. 13–120. I am obliged to Prof. Janovskaja for sending me this important historical treatise along with several other publications.
31. Küng *op. cit.* See also his paper in this volume.
32. A complete report in Ljapunov, A. A.: *Matematičeskie issledovanija, svjazannye s ekspluatacej elektronnyx vyčislitel'nyx mašin*. In: *Matematika v SSSR za sorok let*. Moskva. 1959. There is a Western report on the early stage of discussions on this subject by A. von Weiss: *Logischer Positivismus und Kybernetik im Blickfeld der bolschewistischen Kritik*. In: Freiburger Zeitschrift f. Phil. u. Theol. 1955, 2, 273–295; summary in: Ost-Probleme 1956, 8, 1478–1485.
33. Sobolev, S. L., Kitov, A. I., Ljapunov, A. A.: *Osnovnye čerty kibernetiki*. VF 1955, 4, 136–148. Kol'man, E.: *Čto takoe kibernetika?* VF 1955, 4, 148–159. Frolov, Ju. P.: *Sovremennaja kibernetika i mozg čeloveka*. VF 1956, 3, 116–122. Sobolev, S. L., Ljapunov, A. A.: *Kibernetika i estestvoznanie*. VF 1958, 5, 127–138. Arab-Ogli, E.A.: *Sociologija i kibernetika*. VF 1958, 5, 138–151. Andrjuščenko, M. N.: *Nekotorye filosofskie voprosy kibernetiki*. FN 1959, 3, 96–107. Berg, A. I.: *O nekotoryx problemax kibernetiki*. VF 1960, 5, 51–62.
34. Practically the whole second part of this book (pp. 300–464), with papers of G. N. Povarov, N. E. Kobrinskij and B. A. Traxtenbrot, A. D. Xarkevič, B. M. Rakov, A. N. Jurasov, V. F. D'jačenko and V. G. Lazarev, is devoted to such problems.
35. Viner, N.: *Kibernetika ili upravlenie i svjaz' v životnom i mašine*. Moskva. 1958.
36. Ešbi, U. R.: *Vvedenie v kibernetiku*. Moskva. 1959.
37. *Problemy kibernetiki*. Moskva. 1959.
38. Sokolovskij, Ju. I.: *Kibernetika nastojaščego i buduščego. O "razumnyx" mašinax, iskusstvennyx organax čuvstv, avtomatičeskom perevode knig, matematičeskoj logike i fiziologii nervnoj dejatel'nosti*. Xar'kov. 1959.
39. Here are two instances of such "classical" textbooks. N. I. Kondakov: *Logika*. Moskva. 1954. has the following content: 1. Object and tasks of logic. 2. The principle of identity. 3. The principle of contradiction. 4. The principle of excluded middle. 5. The principle of sufficient reason. 6. Logical procedures. 7. The judgement. 8. The reasoning: Inductive reasoning. 9. Deductive reasoning. 10. Analogy. 11. Hypothesis. 12. The Concept. 13. Relations between the concepts. 14. Demonstration. – The plan of the work is certainly not deprived of a certain originality, but the content is, obviously, quite classical. Another instance is *Logika (pod. red. D. P. Gorskogo i P. V. Tavanca)*. Moskva. 1956: 1. Object and importance of the science of logic. 2. The concept. 3. Logical operation on concepts. 4. The judgement. 5. The kinds *(vidy)* of simple judgement. 6. The kinds of complex judgement. 7. Reasoning. Direct reasoning. 8. The syllogism. 9. Disjunctive and conditional reasoning. Relational reasoning. 10. Inductive reasoning. 11. Methods for the establishment of the causal connection between the phenomena. 12. Analogy. 13. The hypothesis. 14. Proof.

REFERENCES

15. Errors in proof. 16. The basic laws of logic. – Here the arrangement is far more conventional but the content is still the same. It may be further remarked that a definition of mathematical logic which appears in the above-quoted work by Kondakov (p. 481b) could equally well appear in the writings of any Western existentialist philosopher.

40. *Voprosy logiki.* Moskva. 1955. See the articles by L. B. Baženov and E. K. Vojšvillo.
41. *Logičeskie Issledovanija.* Moskva. 1959. See the articles quoted in footnote 22.
42. VF 1959, 3, 175–179.
43. For example, that of Gorskij quoted above.
44. For a statement of the situation and an able presentation of the case for modern logic, see E. Kol'man: *Značenie simboličeskoj logiki.* In: *Logičeskie Issledovanija.* Moskva. 1959 (pp. 3–19).
45. See T. Blakeley: *Soviet Scholasticism* (Sovietica) in print, and his paper in the present volume.
46. See, for example, Mamardašvili, M. K.: *Processy analiza i sinteza.* VF 1958, 2, 50–63.
47. E.g. Kopnin, P. V.: *O xaraktere znanija, soderžaščegosja v gipoteze.* FN 1958, 2, 106–120.
48. See Bocheński *Einführung* pp. 610–611.
49. Novikov *op. cit.* p. 9f.
50. See the papers quoted in notes 15 to 19 and those of E. K. Vojšvillo (pp. 3–31), A. S. Axmanov (32–102), L. B. Baženov (103–119) and V. F. Asmus (192–284) – all in *Voprosy logiki.* Moskva. 1955. The newest relevant contribution is Narskij, I. S.: *K voprosu o sootnošenii formal'noj logiki i dialektiki.* In: Vestnik M-ogo Universiteta 1960, 3, pp. 51–63.
51. Bocheński *loc. cit.*
52. VF 1951, 3, 152–163.
53. Lobkowicz *op. cit.*
54. Bakradze and Kondakov in the articles quoted in 18 and 19.
55. Axmanov, A. S.: *Formy mysli i zakony formal'noj logiki.* In: *Voprosy logiki.* Moskva. 1955 (pp. 32–102) and *Logičeskoe učenie Aristotela.* Moskva. 1956.
56. Aristotel': *Analitiki pervaja i vtoraja.* Moskva. 1952. The older translation dates from 1894.
57. Zinov'ev, A. A.: *O rabote seminara po logike v Institute filosofii AN SSSR.* VF 1958, 2, 167–172.
58. Stjažkin, N. I.: *Elementy algebry logiki i teorii semantičeskix antinomij v pozdnej srednevekovoj logike.* In: *Logičeskie issledovanija.* Moskva. 1959 (pp. 20-32).
59. Primakovskij, A. P.: *Bibliografija po logike. Xronologičeskij ukazatel' proizvedennij po voprosam logiki izdannyx na russkom jazyke v SSSR v XVIII–XX vv.* Moskva. 1955.
60. Kalandaršvili, G. M.: *Očerki po istorii logiki v Gruzii. Materialy i opyt issledovanija.* Tbilisi. 1952.
61. Asmus, V. F.: *Kritika buržuaznyx idealističeskix učenij logiki epoxi imperializma.* In: *Voprosy logiki.* Moskva. 1955 (pp. 192–284).
62. One such study is in preparation by the author.

G. KÜNG

MATHEMATICAL LOGIC IN THE SOVIET UNION

(1917–1947 AND 1947–1957)

On the occasion of the celebration of the 15th, 30th and 40th year of mathematical work in the Soviet Union, detailed reports on the results obtained were published in Moscow. The last report, that published in 1959, is especially extensive – it consists of two large volumes totalling some 1821 pages. The first volume gives the usual reviews of work done in the different branches of mathematics, while the second constitutes a novelty – it contains a practically complete bibliography of Soviet mathematics, 1917 to 1957 [1].

The reports published in 1948 and 1959 each contain a part wholly devoted to mathematical logic [2]. Both were written by S. A. Janovskaja, professor for the history and philosophy of mathematics at the University of Moscow. It is interesting to note the difference in style and content between the two, because this clearly shows the difficulties mathematical logic had to meet from the beginning in the SU and how, nevertheless, it has now developed into a discipline with an independent status in the organization of Soviet science.

We will take first the report of 1948. The part on mathematical logic contains 35 pages of text and is placed under the heading: "Foundations of Mathematics and Mathematical Logic". The first paragraph is concerned with philosophical questions. The author endeavours to demonstrate the "orthodoxy" of Soviet workers in the field of the foundations, and to point out what an important position they are holding in the fight against bourgeois "idealism". In the effort to define a truly Marxist-Leninist view of the philosophy of mathematics, an important role had been played by the edition of the "Mathematical Manuscripts" [3] of Karl Marx and by the comments made on them by S.A. Janovskaja, V. I. Glivenko, L. P. Gokieli, E. Kol'man and others. A distinguishing feature of this first report on mathematical logic are the quotations of the "classics" and even of A. A. Ždanov, secretary of the Central Committee of the Party [4]. The second paragraph of the report of 1948 aims at a justification of mathematical logic. Janovskaja mentions three main points, which should show mathematical logic as acceptable for Soviet science. First, she underlines the recognised merits of Russian logicians (above all of P. S. Poreckij and A. N. Kolmogorov). Then she tries to show the compatibility of Dialectical Materialism and mathematical logic. By referring to the incompleteness of every formalization as demonstrated by Gödel, she refutes the formalist conception which treats mathematics as a mere abacus. In order to reconcile the principle of non-contradiction of formal logic with the dialectical dogma of the contradictory nature of reality, she argues, in connection with the situation of the "liar", "that an interpreted axiomatic system can, nevertheless, be contradictory if we do not take special precautionary measures concerning the formulation of the axioms and the applicable means of logical deduction" (p. 24). The difficulty for her is how to formulate any particular question – if this formulation is well done, then no answers which contradict one another are any longer possible: "to a concrete, rightly *(pravil'no)* formulated question there is only one answer, which is completely determined and unambiguous" (p. 24). A third argument speaking strongly in favour of mathematical logic consists in the fact that the application of mathematical logic in mathematics and in cybernetics is very fruitful.

It is only after this affirmation of the scholars' loyalty to the Party line and of the compatibility, and even utility, of mathematical logic for Dialectical Materialism, that Janovskaja, in a third paragraph, gives a survey of the work done by Soviet logicians up to 1947. She recalls the well-known contributions of A. N. Kolmogorov, V. I. Glivenko and A. Ja. Xinčin on the subject of intuitionism. Further, Janovskaja hails the foundation of combinatory logic by M. I. Schönfinkel as a Soviet discovery because he had been the pupil of S. O. Šatunovskij and had died in Moscow in 1942. The rather precarious position of mathematical logic was strengthened when so deserved a man as Prof. I. I. Žegalkin, an authority in the field of set theory, became interested in logic too. Unfortunately, he died in 1947 before having completed a textbook of mathematical logic. But, at the end of her first report, Janovskaja could already devote nine pages to the respectable achievements of a new generation of logicians (P. S. Novikov, D. A. Bočvar, A. I. Mal'cev, A. A. Markov,[5] etc.). A specialized seminar of mathematical logic had been organized in Moscow, and M. A. Gavrilov and V. I. Šestakov, inspired by the American, S. Shannon, started investigating the logical algebra of relay systems.

Nevertheless, considering the whole period, the author had to admit that the works which gave evidence of a complete understanding of the subject matter were too scarce and that Soviet scholars still had very much to do in this field (p. 45).

In comparison with 1948, where just the start of organized mathematico-logical investigation could be recorded, the situation in 1959 is completely different. This is immediately evident from the inversion of the title – it now runs "Mathematical Logic and the Foundations of Mathematics". Mathematical logic in the Soviet Union is no longer a mere philosophic appendix to mathematics, but has become a recognized branch of science. The reviews for the period 1947–1957, which is a third of the length of the previous period, take up three times as much space (108 pp.). Also, it is no longer necessary as previously to devote two of three paragraphs to the ideological justification of logic and the logicians. The text is now made up entirely of technical reviews where the names of the "classics of Marxism-Leninism" never appear. There is only one place where it is said that the constructive, so-called intuitionist species of mathematics (which is culti-vated by most Russian scholars) has nothing to do with bourgeois "ideal-ism" (pp. 16–17). And in her conclusion, Janovskaja briefly refers to the statement of N. I. Stjažkin: "Dialectical Materialism asks for solution (*razre-šenie*) and not for 'fetishization' (*fetišizacij*) of contradictions"; "dialec-tical contradiction has nothing in common with formal-logical contradic-tion" [6].

Prof. Janovskaja is now able to enumerate a long list of institutions where research in the domain of mathematical logic has been organized. The Institute of Mathematics of the Academy of Sciences has, as of 1957, a special departement for mathematical logic, directed by P. S. Novikov. In Moscow and Leningrad respectively, two genuine "schools" of spe-cialists have arisen, the first centred around the masters A. N. Kolmogo-rov and P. S. Novikov, the second formed by the pupils of A. A. Markov[7]. In several other universities and pedagogical institutes (e. g. in Riga, Ivan-ovo, Penza, Gor'kij, etc.) there are also groups of mathematical logicians. Further, one has to take into account the institutes of related sciences where mathematical logic is studied. Its application to engineering and linguistics is carefully investigated [8]. And among philosophers the question of the relationship between logic and dialectic is still vigorously debated [9]. As for the technical literature in logic, the journal *"Matematika"* has started reviewing Soviet and foreign publications. Further, three important monographs by Soviet logicians have been printed [10] and four of the best foreign textbooks have been translated with – as is the custom in the Soviet Union – valuable introductions [11].

The contributions to logic in the SU have become so numerous that Prof. Janovskaja has to apologize: "It is scarcely possible to give, in a short survey, satisfactory information on the work accomplished and the results obtained" (p. 13). The reviews are distributed in four chapters and thirteen paragraphs (the editing of several paragraphs was able to be left to younger collaborators). The titles of the chapters are: I. Some Questions of Set Theory; II. Theory of Algorithms and Calculable Functions and Operators; III. Mathematical Applications of the Theory of Algorithms; IV. Logical and Logico-Mathematical Calculi.[12]

REFERENCES

1. *Matematika v SSSR za pjatnadcat' let*. Moskva. 1932. *Matematika v SSSR za tridcat' let*. Moskva. 1948. *Matematika v SSSR za sorok let*. Moskva. 1959 (2 vols.).
2. For the bibliography of the works in the field of mathematical logic which are reviewed there, see G. Küng: *A Bibliography of Soviet Mathematical Logic*. Ms. in the Institute of East-European Studies, University of Fribourg, Switzerland.
3. Marx, K.: *Matematičeskie rukopisi*. Moskva. 1932.
4. One must remember that on 24 June 1947, on the occasion of the condemnation of G. F. Aleksandrov's "History of Philosophy in Western Europe", A. A. Ždanov, the son-in-law of Stalin, had addressed the philosophers in a well-known speech where he demanded more active and more belligerent work and, thereby, inaugurated a new period in Soviet philosophy.
5. The logician A. A. Markov (b. 1903) is not to be confused with A. A. Markov (1856–1922), the theoretician of probability.
6. Stjažkin, N. I.: *O logičeskix paradoksax i ix otnošenii k dialektičeskim protivorečijam*. VF 1958, 1, 145–147. Quoted by Janovskaja on pp. 117–118. (Incidentally, the reference given by Janovskaja is false.) As we shall see, what has been said does not mean that philosophers are no longer interested in the question of formal logic – the contrary is the case.
7. Already since 1946 A. V. Kuznecov has kept a record of the proceedings of the seminars in Moscow. A collection of the works of the Leningrad "school" was published as volume 52 of *"Trudy matematičeskogo instituta"* (AN SSSR 1958).
8. The 1959 report on mathematics in the SU contains a special section on cybernetics and this section is not a sub-division of that on mathematical logic.
9. See N. Lobkowicz: *Das Widerspruchsprinzip in der neueren sowjetischen Philosophie* (Sovietica). Dordrecht. 1959 and his paper in the present volume.
10. Markov, A. A.: *Teorija algorifmov*. (1954) Novikov, P. S.: *Ob algoritmičeskoj nerazrešimosti problemy toždestva slov v teorii grupp*. (1955) Šanin, N. A.: *O nekotoryx logičeskix problemax arifmetiki*. (1955)
11. Namely: Hilbert-Ackerman, Tarski, Kleene (see notes 25, 26 and 27 in "Soviet Logic" in this volume) and Péter, R.: *Rekursivnye funkcii*. Moskva. 1954.
12. After this article had been written, the author learned, through the kindness of Dr. Buchholz, that a paper by V. Richter, *"Mathematische Logik in der Sowjetunion"*, is forthcoming in "Osteuropa-Naturwissenschaft".

THE PRINCIPLE OF CONTRADICTION IN
RECENT SOVIET PHILOSOPHY *

The meeting "On the Questions of Dialectical Contradictions in the Light of Contemporary Science and Practice", organized by the Institute of Philosophy of the Academy of Sciences of the USSR and held in Moscow in April of 1958, is noteworthy from several points of view even for those who do not normally occupy themselves with questions of Marxism-Leninism. *First*, to judge from the reports received, this meeting was remarkably objective. Several of the addresses gave evidence of a definite impartiality, unusual in the Soviet context. In the *second* place, this is the first time that Soviet philosophers have systematically discussed the "dialectical" contradiction, which is the most significant aspect of the Hegelian heritage of their philosophy. Although Hegel's name appears very seldom, it is evident that the participants form two groups: those who defend the "dialectical" contradiction, "dialectical" logic, in a word, the legacy of Hegel as transmitted by Engels and Lenin; and those who defend formal logic, try to interpret "real" contradictions as polar oppositions and for whom "Hegelian" is almost an insult. Without a doubt, the "strategic" position of the first group is much more favourable since its members can almost invariably count on the support of the "classics", who prized contradiction and "dialectical" logic very highly. The partisans of the second group find themselves in a particularly uncomfortable situation since they must either bring their defence of reason and logic into agreement with the statements of the "classics" or contradict these same "classics". That this last possibility actually was realized is the *third* and most noteworthy fact about the meeting.

The following is a general view of the opinions defended at this meeting:

(1) All of the speakers agreed that there are real contradictions. Even those who criticised the current definition of these contradictions (E. Kolman) or the law of the unity and conflict of opposites (N. V. Karabanov) had in

* Lobkowicz, N.: *Das Widerspruchsprinzip in der neueren sowjetischen Philosophie* (Sovietica Veröffentlichungen 4). Dordrecht. 1959.

view, in the final analysis, purely terminological and not real difficulties. But there was a real difference of opinion as to *what* a real contradiction really is: some (e.g. S. P. Dudel', N. V. Karabanov, E. V. Il'enkov, etc.) had in mind the (Hegelian) version of Engels in the sense of a mutual inter-penetration (i.e. the simultaneous and mutual self-position and self-negation of contrary or even contradictorily opposed "aspects" of the object); others, however, and Kolman above all, spoke simply of the conjunction of various polar-opposed (in certain circumstances) forces or tendencies. However, the positions on this point were none too clear and there was a certain slippage in the sense that under "real contradiction" were subsumed things as different as "position-negation" and "North-Pole – South-Pole" – the distinction, common among Western logicians, between contradictory, contrary, sub-contrary and polar oppositions was not once mentioned.

(2) The real parting of the ways came on the question as to how real contradictions are conceived in thought. Certain speakers such as E. V. Il'enkov were of the opinion that, in certain cases, contradictory formulations are not only technically unavoidable, but even true. In opposition to this, the logicians present stressed that contradictory judgements are false in all cases, and A. A. Zinov'ev was more definite when he said that they can represent nothing which is in reality. M. K. Mamardašvili took this opportunity to point out that it didn't matter if the object in question contained real contradictions or not. This last assertion seems to create a dilemma: if contradictory judgements are false in all cases, then one must either deny that the reality in question is really contradictory (as did Kolman) or take refuge in an even more curious "conceptualism". We find such a "conceptualism" in, to cite only one instance, the" *Osnovy marksistskoj filosofii"*, where it is said on page 256 that Aristotle had correctly formulated the principle of contradiction of formal logic, but that he had erroneously inferred that the real could not be contradictory. In other words, the conjunction of two mutually contradictory propositions is always false and, in spite of this, it does not follow that one and the same thing cannot have two mutually contradictory properties. It is easy to understand why this assertion is not further justified – it is based on the dogmatic assertion that there are real contradictions – for it is hardly possible to give a rational foundation to such an assertion.

(3) Further, a few theses were defended which, even if not completely "unorthodox", were at least new. The concept of *"ravnodejstvie"*, "the

resultant", introduced by N. V. Karabanov, seems to have met with universal approval, while the standpoint of C. A. Stepanjan, according to which there are "contradictions" which contain not real oppositions but simple differences of nature, was rejected as inconsequent. Doomed to remain in suspense was the thesis, proposed by V. M. Kvačaxija, which presented contradictions as obstacles to development instead of as its source.[1]

(4) The veritable sensation of the meeting, however, was without any doubt the address of E. Kolman, who took it upon himself to put an assertion of one of the "classics" to a critical examination – a rare happening in the history of *Soviet* Diamat.[2] Therefore, we will pay particular attention to E. Kolman and to the development which made possible and permitted his criticism.

(a) E. Kolman (b. 6 December 1882 in Prague) is Czech by birth (this is why we write his name "Kolman" and not "Kol'man", which is the Russian form of it; "E." is the Russian transcription of "Arnošt", i.e. "Ernest"); near the end of the first World War he was taken prisoner by the Russians and did not return at the end of the war. From 23 December 1939 on he was a full professor in Moscow and, as of 1 November 1945, he was professor in Prague – but, already in 1948 he went back to Moscow (rumour has it, because of conflict with the Czech Communist Party). Later Kolman became professor at the Moscow Institute for the History of Science and Technology; to-day he is director of the Institute of Philosophy of the Czechoslovak Academy of Sciences.[3]

Kolman came to philosophy through the empirical sciences and he belongs to the small, but influential, group of those Soviet philosophers who have long since rejected any subordination of the empirical sciences to "philosophical" dogmas. It was Kolman who in 1948 – therefore, only a year after the appearance of the *"Voprosy filosofii"* and before the beginning of the Soviet logic discussion – published (in Prague) a "critical presentation" of mathematical logic [4]. A glance at the bibliography and Name-Index shows that the relevant literature from Leibniz, through Frege, Boole, Peano, Russell-Whitehead, up to Łukasiewicz, Tarski, Church, Quine, etc., is not only known to him but valued by him – something which was, at that time, really unusual. Later we find Kolman as one of the first defenders [5] of the originally despised cybernetics,[6] to which he devoted a book some years ago [7]. In 1955 he published a work on B. Bolzano which is of interest even to Western readers [8]. Furthermore, Kolman seems to be much more familiar with the ancients than the majority of Soviet philosophers – he is probably the sole philosopher in the Soviet Union who introduced, word for word, the Aristotelian definition of quantity and, what is more, who saw that before the Marxists no one, Hegel included, had said anything more intelligible on this topic [9]. And his next little venture (on Anaximander) is in the same line.

(b) Since, as S. P. Dudel' pointed out during the discussion in question, Kolman is dependent on the Polish Marxist, A. Schaff, we must clarify this point. In 1946, at a time when (as is again the case, in a certain sense, now) there was in Poland living and free philosophic discussion, A. Schaff published an article on the principle of contradiction in the light of dialectical logic, in which he, in order to be able to explain movement dialectically, denies, for all practical purposes, the principle of contradiction [10]. Impressed by arguments of non-Marxist Polish thinkers (above all of the logician and philosopher, K. Ajdukiewicz [11], Schaff found himself forced to revise his opinion. In 1955 he wrote an article in which he recognized the validity of the principle of contradiction and rejected the thesis on the contradictory nature of movement as false [12]. In this article, Schaff begins with an analysis of the word "is", which he says has caused so much "bother" *(niejednego figla)* in philosophic disputes. He accepts from Ajdukiewicz the version which originated with A. Reinach (a German phenomenologist) and according to which "is", when applied to local motion, can mean as well "happen" as "reach", "leave" or "stay" – but Schaff reduces these four to two: that a body is at a certain point can mean that the body rests *(spoczywać)* at that point or passes it *(mijać)*. If a body rests in a place, then it does not move. If one means with "is" that the body passes a point, it is evident that, on the one hand, the body is viewed as "moving" but, on the other hand, it is obvious that it then either passes or does not pass – certainly not both at the same time. There is a contradiction only, then, when one confuses "is" as "passes" with "is" as "rests". The Eleatics thought that an arrow in flight was at rest in each instant of its flight, whereby rest was made absolute and movement impossible. With this version in mind, the statement that a body moves leads, of course, to a contradiction. Marx and Engels (and, from them, Lenin) had inherited this false posing of the problem from Hegel, who, for his part, recognized movement as something objective and, nevertheless, held the Eleatic conception of movement as a series of rest-points. Schaff himself espoused this version later,[13] even in the face of numerous attacks. According to the Soviet philosopher, M. N. Alekseev,[14] Schaff can no longer give any explanation of movement, if its nature consists in the fact that a body is, and at the same time is not, at a certain point. And the Pole, J. Ładosz, points out that the thesis on the contradictory nature of movement is indispensable for the explanation of its source and possibility [15]. In reference to the last argument, shortly before this the Pole, H. Eilstein, stressed in a much-discussed article [16] that if movement is an existential form of matter, then a question as to the source and possibility of movement is as senseless as a question of the type, "Why is the world material?", "Why does an event follow laws?" Later, we find this discussion in other satellites. Thus, H. Ley in Eastern Germany thoroughly investigated the arguments used by Ajdukiewicz against Schaff [17]. In Czechoslovakia, in the Spring of 1957, we find the theme taken up by J. Bartoš [18], a philosopher who attacked the doctrine of the negation of negation [19] a year later and had a public discussion with B. M. Kedrov in this reference [20]. Bartoš argued as follows: Zeno and Hegel presuppose that, if there is really movement, the moving body is, in one and the same instant, at one point and at another. While Zeno concludes to the impossibility of movement, for Hegel (and, through him, for Engels and later for Lenin) movement is a basic philosophical category to which he blindly sacrifices the principle of contradiction. According to Bartoš the Eleatics had not only solved the problem wrongly but also posed it falsely. For, when one speaks of an instant, one abstracts from duration, hence from motion itself – in an instant nothing can move. Therefore, when we speak of an instant, then we should not speak of the body being in motion and vice versa. If one wishes to maintain that "instant" can also indicate an infinitesimal duration, then one must remember that in this case the body accomplishes an infinitesimal movement. In any case, one cannot, in the same thought-process, take an instant as an abstraction from time ("the body is at rest at a point") and as a small duration ("and yet it moves"). "Otherwise, of course, there is a contradiction but only in our thinking and not at all in the reality around us." Finally, Bartoš comes out against the Leninist thesis according to which movement is a contradiction because there is a unity of continuity and discontinuity, and he is content to here point out that this thesis is for the most part nothing but a "simple phrase" – in order to argue against it, one must first find rational arguments that might in some way support it. This most ingenious and pointedly written article evoked a discussion in Czechoslovakia which to this day continues [21] and in which Bartoš himself took further part [22].

Now, back to Kolman. It is certain that he does not go as far as Schaff and Bartoš but, on the other hand, it should not be overlooked that he traces Engels' misunderstanding of the relationship between higher and lower mathematics to his denial of the "categoricity of thought" and, in a corollary, indicates that there are things in the "Dialectics of Nature" with which the mathematician and scientist cannot be in agreement. Apart from this, we find in his address a strong functionalist tendency (reduction of the basic contradictions of matter to contradictions between "physical" properties; repeated protest against the absolutization of scientific theories, etc.) and an unusual, positive appreciation of Western researchers (Heisenberg and even Eddington). In conclusion, one can say that, *mutatis mutandis*, his address could as well have been delivered by a Western physicist or philosopher.

REFERENCES

1. E. T. Lukina had already espoused a similar version in VF 1957, 3, 132–136.
2. More precisely, we know of only two such cases. The first is that of E. A. Asratjan (VF 1955, 5, 36; whereto, see A. G. Rudov, VF 1956, 6, 217 and A. S. Piette, VF 1956, 2, 236f.) who attacked a statement of Engels on the direct relationship of sensations with "certain albuminous bodies". The second is that of Kolman, treated here.
3. *Adresář učitelských sil a vědeckých ústavů university Karlovy v Praze 1946/47*. Praha. 1946. (p. 38).
4. E. Kolman: *Kritický výklad symbolické metody moderní logiky*. Praha. 1948. The oldest publication by Kolman known to us is *Predmet i metod sovremennoj matematiky*. Moskva. 1936, later in: *Učebnik logiki*. Moskva. 1942. In addition to these, Kolman published in Czech: *Ideologie německého fašizmu*. Praha. 1946; *Přednášky o základech vědecké filosofie*. Praha. 1947; as editor (with an article on the relationship of philosophy to non-Euclidean geometry, pp. 102–115) *"Vzestup"*, *Sborník marxistických studií*. Praha. 1948.
5. E. Kolman: *Čto takoe kibernetika?* VF 1955, 4, 148–159.
6. See Materialist: *Komu služit kibernetika*. VF 1953, 5, 210–219; S. Bogusławski, H. Greniewski, J. Szapiro: *Dialogi o cybernetice*. Myśl Filozoficzna 1954, 4, 158–212; a Czech article in *"Za socialistickou vědu a techniku"* 1952, no. 4–5. Among the Western articles which are noticed in the East there is A. Lentin: *La cybernétique, problèmes réels et mystification*. In: La Pensée 1953(47), 47–61.
7. Czech translation: A. Kolman: *Kybernetika*. Praha. 1957. The Russian original was not available.
8. E. Kolman: *Bernard Bolzano*. Moskva. 1955. Further: *Velikij russkij myslitel N. I. Lobačevskij*. Iz. 2. Moskva. 1956.
9. See *Filosofický časopis*. Praha. 1957, 3, 443 – it is an address, held in Moscow in 1955, on categories.
10. Schaff, A.: *Zasada sprzeczności w świetle logiki dialektycznej*. In: Myśl Współczesna 1946, 3–4.
11. Ajdukiewicz, K.: *Zmiana i sprzeczność*. In: Myśl Współczesna 1948, 8–9; see also St. Ossowski: *Na szlakach marksizmu. ibid.*
12. Schaff, A.: *Dialektyka marksistowska a zasada spreczności*. In: Myśl Filozoficzna 1955, 4.
13. See, for example, *O dialektyce i zasadzie logicznej sprzeczności*. In: Studia Filozoficzne 1957, 1.
14. Alekseev, M. N.: *O dialektičeskoj prirode suždenija*. VF 1956, 2, 56.
15. Ładosz, J.: *O sprzecznościach logicznych i dialektycznych*. In: Myśl Filozoficzna 1956, 4. See also W. Rolbiecki: *Niektóre zagadnienia logiki formalnej w świetle teorii marksizmu-leninizmu*. In: Myśl Filozoficzna 1955, 2.
16. Eilstein, H.: *Logika w świetle marksistowskej teorii poznania*. In: *ibid.* 1956, 2.
17. Ley, H.: *Über Fragen der Logik*. In: Deutsche Zeitschrift für Phil. 1956, 4.
18. Bartoš, J.: *Paradoxní these o rozpornosti pohybu a problém zásad správného myšlení*. In: Filosofický časopis. Praha. 1957, 3, 340–357.
19. Bartoš, J.: *O tzv. zákonu negace negace*. In: Filosofický časopis 1958, 2, 268–281.
20. See the report in *Filosofický časopis* 1959, 4, 636–640. The discussion took place on 12 Nov. 1958 in Prague when Kedrov was there.

21. See P. Materna: *Ještě k paradoxům, logice a dialektice*. In: Filosofický časopis 1957, 6, 877–879; Mlíkovský, Vl.: *K pojetí pohybu v marxistické filosofii*. ibid. 1959, 3, 359–370; Zd. Javůrek: *Několik poznámek k diskusi o vztahu principu nespornosti a dialektiky*. ibid. 1959, 5, 724–730.

22. J. Bartoš: *O rozporech v myšlení*. In: Filosofický časopis 1958, 4, 581–587.

SOVIET PHILOSOPHY'S CONCEPTION OF
"BASIC LAWS", "ORDER"* AND "PRINCIPLES"

Some time ago the "Bulletin of the University of Moscow" published an article, "On the Question of the Classification of the Basic Laws of the Dialectic and their Inter-Connection", in which S. P. Lebedev gave a polemic accent to the philosophical differences of opinion due to the acceptance by some of Stalin's interpretation of Diamat and the return to tradition – made possible by Stalin's death – of others. According to Lebedev, there is "insufficient clarity on the classification of the basic laws of the materialist dialectic as well in the textbooks on Dialectical Materialism and single articles as in pedagogic practice." The Marxist dialectical method is so presented in the textbooks that one has the impression that in nature and society and, also, in thought not three but four basic laws of the dialectic are operative. This impression is due to the fact that the authors of the textbooks present all four traits of the Marxist dialectical method as basic laws of the dialectic.[1] When one takes into account that these textbooks include the law of the negation of negation among the basic laws [2], then it becomes clear how this classification differs from that held by the "classics of Marxism-Leninism". It is well known that the founders of the materialist dialectic, critically developing the entire progressive content of philosophy and science, formulated three basic laws of the materialist dialectic: the law of the unity and battle of opposites; the law of the transition of quantity into quality and vice versa; and the law of the negation of negation [3]. These basic principles are, as a matter of fact, examined in the textbooks without any justification. And they are given another structure – a structure corresponding to the four basic characteristics [4] of the Marxist dialectical method [5] – whereby the transformation which marked the high point

---

* Translator's note: The German word *Gesetzmässigkeit* (for the Russian *zakonomernost'*) has, at least in certain contexts, no exact equivalent in English. It designates that order, regularity or uniformity which is the basis of a law. Thus, the "Law of Gravity" is based on the observation of a certain order or regularity in physical events, e.g. in the fall of objects or parabolic flight of projectiles. Therefore, we have variously translated *Gesetzmässigkeit* as "order", "regularity" or "uniformity", as the context and sentence-structure demanded.

of the Stalinist epoch is simply accepted. Here, "there is no basic trait of the Marxist dialectical method which does not reflect a basic law of the objective dialectic"[6]. S. Ja. Kogan once argued that on the basis of this assumption "the unification of the first and second groups of elements of the dialectic leads directly to a doctrine of five basic traits or (basic) laws of the materialist dialectic: (1) The general connectivity, mutual determination and unity of phenomena of nature and society; (2) Movement and development in nature and society; (3) Development as transition of quantitative changes into qualitative; (4) Development as battle of opposites. As a result of the exclusion of the 'Negation of Negation' (5) from the basic traits or laws of the dialectic, one finds a doctrine on the four basic traits of the dialectical method, which fully corresponds to the classification used in Comrade Stalin's work"[7]. Lebedev and the majority of his fellow faculty members [8] have another point of view. For him, the editing of the presentation from the "Dialectics of Nature" (see *Dialektika prirody*. Moskva. 1950. p. 1) in reference to its scientific bases is unacceptable, since for him "it seems that there are no such bases. Engels was right not to put the principles of universal connection and development among the basic laws of the dialectic"[9]. For "in the objective world, the endlessly numerous connections and movements, transformations, of phenomena supply only the sphere, the *sine qua non*, of the working of the dialectic's basic laws"; while, finally, "the movement and development and, therefore, the inter-connection of phenomena, determine the world"[10]. Lebedev tries to refute Kogan's quasi-idealistic "false proof" that "the doctrine on movement and development of natural and social phenomena forms the heart of the doctrine on inter-connection and mutual determination"[11] – or, in the words of his critic, "forms the basis of the universal interconnectivity of phenomena"[12] – with an equally unjustified assumption as to the indivisibility of the uniform world-process in which "the connection of the phenomena" would be "movement itself"[13]. But he has no success in explaining exactly how his statement differs from that of Kogan; for, if movement is the connection of phenomena, then the simple presence of the beings and their essences is enough to bring into existence the necessary attribute of determination, which is, in fact, equivalent to a confirmation of Kogan's view. Further, this consequence is implied by the interpretation of Lebedev himself according to which "the general principle of development is organically connected with the general principle of the unity of the world or with the principle of general connection"." These two principles, which could be called, in a certain sense, constants, express one and the same state of affairs, i.e. that there are no phenomena in reality which are not in movement and development." On this basis it is further the case "that movement and change, together with inter-connection, are the integrating form of the existence of matter. But these laws – if the word can be used in this context – are not to be projected onto the level of the basic laws of the dialectic nor put in the same series with them. It is more a question here of different laws which are distinguished both as regards the range of characteristics and as regards the profundity and specific mode of reflecting reality. The first laws, which we expressly term the primary principles of the dialectic as science, are only expressions of the generality of the movement and inter-connection of phenomena. In contradistinction to these, the basic laws of the dialectic reflect not only the 'generality of the form' but also and at the same time the essential and necessary relationships. What is more, each of these basic laws of the dialectic expresses a definite and specific internal connection in the development of phenomena and serves to qualify the development in this or that relationship" [14].

For some time now the so-called "fundamental traits of Marxist philosophic materialism" have been designated, in Soviet technical literature, as the basic laws of this philosophy. V. P. Tugarinov [15], one of the leading thinkers of the post-Stalinist era, took a stand on this much disputed question in his book on "The Laws of the Objective World, Their Understanding and Use" (1954): "The laws of the Marxist dialectic have always been and always will be operative. The same is true of the laws of Marxist philosophic materialism, which reveal the most general *relationship* between being and consciousness" [16]. From which Lebedev draws the conclusion – undoubtedly valid on materialist assumptions – that this statement implies the eternal existence and operativity of consciousness as a specific force [17] – but this is a categorical denial of one of the positive norms of Soviet philosophy. Further, Lebedev energetically attacks Tugarinov's opinion where he stresses that one must "speak here of the fundamental *principles* of philosophic materialism" because the "scientifically" established matter of fact that "the world is essentially material" and "matter is the sole objective reality which exists independent of our consciousness (cannot) be considered as a law. Those comrades who take this basic principle for a law have in mind the fact that a very important characteristic of a general law is present – i.e. the generality – since *all* phenomena in the world are material. But one cannot forget that every law, in the strict sense of the word, expresses a necessary *relationship*. If this relationship is general as basis of movement, of development, for this or that group of phenomena, then one can speak of a law. In the present instance, however, when we formulate the first characteristic of Marxist philosophic materialism, we fix the most general property of all phenomena – their materiality – but not the essential relationships between the properties, aspects and objects. Hence, there are a great number of propositions in which the general nature of one or another characteristic of objects is determined or fixed but which cannot be taken as laws in the strict sense of the term".[18] The same is true of the primacy of matter over consciousness and the intelligibility of being. These are principles and not laws of Marxist philosophy for, in the first case, there is a specific relation which is not a mutually necessary relationship of two phenomena which determine a common development or even existence as a whole [19], while in the other case it is a question "simply of the characteristic of *one property*, i.e. the capacity of the consciousness to know the world around it" [20].

Schematically, what we have seen up to now on the basic laws, order and principles of Dialectical Materialism can be represented as follows:

Principles of Philosophic Materialism

(1) The materiality, objective reality and independence from consciousness of being.
(2) The priority of Matter over consciousness.
(3) The reflection of being in consciousness.

Principles (Uniformities/Regularities) of the Dialectic

(1) General movement and development of being and knowing.
(2) The unity of the world and connectivity of its phenomena.

Basic Laws of the Dialectic

(1) Unity and battle of opposites.
(2) Transition of quantity into quality.
(3) Negation of negation or spiral development.

Leading Soviet philosophers give various precisions as to the essence of these general determinations, but the differences leave the heart of the materialist dialectic undisturbed. So far as "principle" is concerned, it has for a short time now played the ontological role of an "οὐσία" and, as such, attracted the attention of the systematic philosophers [21]. The basic source is adequately provided by Engels' well known presentation in "Anti-Düh-ring": "Principles (are) not the point of departure of the investigation but its result; they are not applied to nature and human history but, rather, abstracted from them; nature and the realm of man do not follow the principles, rather the principles are correct only in so far as they correspond to nature and history. This is the only materialist version of the matter" [22]. In his book "The Marxist-Leninist Dialectic as Philosophical Science", V. P. Rožin (University of Leningrad) designates principles, with reference to this text, as "basic guiding lines without which the construction of the theory and method of every science is impossible" [23]. They are, however, "not a product of human imagination but the reflection of the ties and relations of the external world"; they "are based on the results of all sciences and the practical activity of mankind" [24]: they are the basis of both the objective and subjective dialectic [25]. P. V. Kopnin (Univ. of Kiev), too, sees the principle as "the fundamental point of departure of a theory, of a doctrine" [26]. He distinguishes scientific principles from the concepts "reg-ularity" and "law" as "regularities which extend over extraordinarily extensive spheres and are the bases of various branches of sciences or even of science itself ... The principle can, therefore, gather a group of laws into a united whole because it reflects a more general law which fixes the essential aspect of the entire process and reveals the peculiar character of this process" [27]. Especially noteworthy is Kopnin's attempt to give to the concept "idea"[28] – heavily over-loaded by Hegel's dialectical idealism [29] – its ontological and epistemological place in contemporary Soviet philoso-phy [30]. "The concepts 'principle' and 'idea' belong to the same order, to the same system, to the extent that they both express fundamental regularities of science. The relationship between the principle and the idea can be ex-pressed as follows: every scientific principle reveals the content of a scientif-ic idea. It appears as a possible determination of the idea in question without, however, exhausting its entire content. On the other hand, not every idea comes to the fore in the principles; for principles are the points of departure of a very general scientific theory, of a branch of science, while, on the contrary, the idea is basic to any theory whatsoever – even a very narrow one – provided that it has a system of knowledge at its service. Further, idea and principle are differentiated by their epistemological function: while the principle is the point of departure of a general scientific theory and the presentation of the theory begins with the principles, the idea, as a basic synthesising principle, is the unconditional prerequisite of every theory. Its principal epistemological function consists in the unification of concepts into a definite system. The scientific theory can be built on two or more principles, but has only one idea, the differentiated content of which is explained by the different principles. As a result, the idea is a special type of concept. A concept which reflects a law is an idea when it has a definite function in the designing and construction of a scientific theory – a function which consists in the fact that it unites the other concepts in a definite system and thus constructs a complete and concrete picture of the objects and processes studied"[31].

In contrast to the conceptual analyses of the most formal systematic position of "idea" and "principle", Soviet philosophic literature on the categories "law" and "regularity" is so rich that it is advisable to limit our consideration to the most important texts. G. F. Aleksandrov defines law as "an essential, self-repetitive and, under certain conditions, constant and very definite tendency of the course (of development) of a limited relationship between phenomena"[32]. This relationship has both an ontological (and that *a priori*) and epistemological *(a posteriori)* character. This means: "The laws of nature and society which are reflected in human consciousness by means of various concepts are laws of science. They express the regularities of processes which take place independent of man"[33]. P. V. Kopnin devotes a section ("Law as a Form of the Connection of Phenomena") of the sixth chapter of the "Principles of Marxist Philosophy" *(Osnovy)* to the interpretation of this correlation. Here, law is "in its most general form ... a definite and necessary relation between things, phenomena or processes – a relation which results from their internal nature, from their essence"[34]. Kopnin, following the line of thought of his previously quoted and earlier investigation of "The Idea and its Role in Knowledge", here draws attention to the fact that the terms "law" and "regularity" (express) relationships of the same order. Hence, they are often used interchangeably. But there is a certain difference. Law is the concrete and necessary relation between phenomena ... The term "regularity" is used, above all, for designating a certain order and sequence of phenomena". But in a strict philosophical sense it denotes "a necessary, causally determined process in which not only one law but a complete totality of laws can be operative"[35]. A comparison of the texts of Rozental'-Štraks, Tugarinov and Rožin shows that the precise definition of law – "this internal and necessary correlation between two apparent contradictories"[36] – has, in more recent special investigations, been more closely determined by four qualifications. They are: essentiality, necessity, generality and relative stability of the relationship [37]. As previously indicated (Kopnin), there is a concern for the epistemological and ontological establishment of the deductive succession "principle (regularity) – law". Rožin writes: "The recognition of the general connection and development of the phenomena of the external world represents the most important basic principle of the materialist dialectic. Law is the form of the general connections of phenomena. From this it follows that the general connection cannot itself be a law. The laws of the dialectic are laws of development; therefore, development cannot itself be a law. In our literature not only are scientific principles confused with the laws of science but also laws are identified with uniformities. This is the cause of disorder and misunderstanding"[38]. Tugarinov, anticipating Rožin's criticism of this terminological confusion in his theory of categories [39], treats laws as concretizations of uniformity. "For science it is not enough to simply discover the general regularities. It develops the principles concerning uniformity further, by unfolding the various aspects of this regularity. Law is nothing else but the exposure of the single aspects of uniformity. Regularity is like a bud out of which the flower with its petals develops. The laws are these petals (which are) developed out of uniformity or regularity"[40]. For Tugarinov the result of the application of this comparison to the theory of existential modes is that "the plurality of philosophic categories ... express the most general uniformities of reality". But, if this is so, "then the relationship between uniformity and law remains indistinct to the extent that law is a combination of categories. There is a contradiction; for, on the one hand, it seems that there is no difference between a category and a law because the categories are themselves uniformities. On the other hand, we form these categories into a law, e.g. into the law of transition of quantity into quality. The way out of this situation consists in being careful not to confuse regularity and law and to avoid completely identifying them. The categories express uniformities while the groups of categories, propositions about categories, are laws. Causality, form, content, etc., represent regularities; the combination of them or propositions about them represent laws . . . If we do not understand this, then we will hardly be able to grasp the correlation of the categories and laws of Dialectical Materialism, we will not be able to understand that law is not on the same level as regularity but rather that it is a matter of distinct epistemological levels, that the law represents a more concrete and more profound level of knowledge than that of the regularities, and it reveals the regularity. It is, indeed, true that the law is more restricted than the regularity because it represents only certain aspects of the regularity but, in comparison to uniformity, it reaches deeper into reality because it makes the uniformity concrete, acts as its foundation and exposes its various aspects."[41]

If we keep in mind the thesis of Engels – developed by Lenin in his study of empiriocriticism – that the principles (viz. regularities) and, of course, the laws of Dialectical Materialism are abstracted, in the course of practical activity, from nature and human history [42] – then what we have seen to be taking place in contemporary Soviet philosophy in this context has a special significance. On the one hand, there is more clarity in reference to the thesis on the primacy of matter over consciousness (i.e. the second principle of philosophic materialism) and, on the other, a contribution to the understanding of the conception of practice as the basis of the dialectico-materialist epistemology and as its absolute criterion of truth.

REFERENCES

1. See, e.g., Aleksandrov, G. F. (ed.): *Dialektičeskij materializm*. Moskva. 1954. (pp. 69ff. and 117ff.)

2. See: Kedrov, B. M.: *Zakon otricanija otricanija*. Kommunist 1956, 13. On the same theme: Vorob'ev, M. F. and Kazakevič, T. A.; Abolenceva, A. G. and El'meev, V. Ja.; Kazakov, A. P., Xarin, Ju. A. and Savel'ev, S. G. – in "*Vestnik Leningradskogo Universiteta. Serija ekonomiki, filosofii, prava*" (henceforward: V LGU SEFP) 1956, 23. Xarin, Ju. A. in V LGU SEFP 1957, 5. Morozov, V. D. in FN 1958, 4. Vorob'ev, M. F.: *Zakon otricanija otricanija*. Leningrad. 1956. Kedrov, B. M.: *Otricanie otricanija*. Moskva. 1957. – See also: Dahm, H.: *Ontologische Aspekte der sowjetischen Dialektik*. In: Osteuropa (Stuttgart) 1957, 4, 233–244.

3. See the discussion on "Programming of the Study-Plan for Dialectical and Historical Materialism" in "*Vestnik vysšej školy*" (VVŠ) and "*Voprosy filosofii*", most of the articles of which are devoted to these three laws and an interpretation of Engels' arrangement of them. In particular: Enevič, F. F. (Kiev) in VVŠ 1957, 1, 28–35. Rutkevič, M. N. (Sverdlovsk) in VVŠ 1957, 4, 36–40. Kazakov, A. P. and Rožin, V. P. (Leningrad) in VVŠ 1957, 4, 40–44. Mixajlov, V. N. (Saratov) in VVŠ 1957, 5, 18–20. Eričev, L. I. (Leningrad) in VVŠ 1957, 5, 21–25. Askinadze, Ja. F. (Saratov) in VVŠ 1957, 6, 17–20. Karasev, B. A. (Murmansk) in VVŠ 1957, 6, 20–24. Zbandut, G. P. (Odessa) in VVŠ 1957, 6, 24–27. as well as thirteen other participants in the discussion (VVŠ 1957, 6, 27–35). Majzel', I. A., Meleščenko, Ju. S., Novikov, A. I. (Leningrad) in VF 1957, 1, 214–216. Kaltaxčjan, S. T. in VF 1958, 2, 162–167. Čaplygina, S. G. (Sverdlovsk) in VF 1958, 4, 175–177. Suslov, I. A., Šubnjakov, B. P., Sidorkin, V. A., Pilipenko, N. V., Šadrin, E. I. (Jaroslavl') in VF 1958, 6, 157–160. Sternin, A. O. (Jaroslavl') in VF 1958, 9, 164–168.

4. (1) General connection between phenomena in nature and society, (2) Movement and development in nature and society, (3) Development as the transition of quantitative changes into qualitative, (4) Development as battle of opposites (see *Kratkij filosofskij slovar'* p. 322 and Wetter, G. A.: *Dialectical Materialism*. London. 1958. p. 310ff.).

5. Lebedev, S. P.: *K voprosu o klassifikacii osnovnyx zakonov dialektiki i ix vzaimosvjazi* In: V MGU SEFP 1958, 2, 80.

6. Kogan, S. Ja. in "*Izvestija Odesskogo gosudarstvennogo universiteta*" (IOGU) 1949, 1, 7.

7. *loc. cit.*

8. See: Enevič, F. F.: VVŠ 1957, 1, 31 and Kazakov, A. P., Rožin V. P.: VVŠ 1957, 4, 42.

9. Lebedev *op. cit.* p. 80.

10. *ibid.* p. 81.

11. Kogan *op. cit.* p. 13.

12. Lebedev *op. cit.* p. 83.

13. *ibid.*

14. *ibid.* ff.

15. Vasilij Petrovič Tugarinov (b. 1899 at Ostaškov in Tver'); began his university studies in 1917 (2 months in Moscow); drafted into the Red Army in 1918 and fought on the Eastern front against the Czechs and Kolčak; 1920 saw the resumption of his studies in Moscow; in 1925 he graduated and joined the Communist Party; from 1925 to 1951 he taught the history of the CPSU and Historical Materialism at

"BASIC LAWS", "ORDER" AND "PRINCIPLES"

Orexovo-Zuevo, Kolomna, Rjazan' and Kalinin; in 1940 he became "Candidate" with a dissertation *"Marksistsko-leninskoe učenie o morali"* and in 1951 a Ph. D. with a dissertation *"Dialektičeskij materializm o zakone i zakonomernosti"*; at the end of 1951 he became Dean of the Faculty of Philosophy and professor of Dialectical and Historical Materialism at the University of Leningrad; he has devoted himself principally to the construction of an ontologically founded theory of categories. Since 1926 he has published a total of 75 scientific works, the most interesting of which are three of the most recent: *Zakony ob'ektivnogo mira, ix poznanie i ispol'zovanie.* Leningrad. 1954. *Sootnošenie kategorij dialektičeskogo materializma.* Leningrad. 1956. *Sootnošenie kategorij istoričeskogo materializma.* Leningrad. 1958. For his biography, see V LGU SEFP 1959, 11, 158.

16. Tugarinov *Zakony* p. 108.
17. See Lebedev *op. cit.* p. 85.
18. Lebedev *op. cit.* p. 84. It should be noted that Tugarinov rejects this view. According to his *Zakony,* every proposition in which a characteristic is attributed to an object – like "All elephants have trunks" – is a law (see p. 133). For all that, Tugarinov's interpretation agrees with the Soviet variation on the doctrine of attributive judgement *(suždenie prinadležnosti)* according to which "The *relations* of identity and difference are reflected in every *judgement,* no matter what its content be. This peculiarity of the judgement of inherence is due to the fact that in its conception we include only that content which is proper to every judgement, i.e. the inherence or non-inherence of a property in an object and the corresponding identity or difference of the objects" (Gorskij, D. P., Tavanec, P. V.: *Logika.* Moskva. 1956, pp. 72 and 104). See also: Asmus, V. F.: *Logika.* Moskva 1947 (pp. 69–76). Gorskij, D. P.: *Logika.* Moskva. 1954 (pp. 46–49). Tavanec, P. V.: *Voprosy teorii suždenija.* Moskva. 1955 (pp. 19–22).
19. Lebedev *op. cit.* p. 84.
20. *ibid.* p. 85.
21. In the standard works, the concept *"zakonomernost'"* (regularity) does not yet have a systematizing function in a theory of principles. See: Rozental', M. M., Judin, P. F.: *Kratkij filosofskij slovar'.* Moskva. 1954. Aleksandrov, G. F. (ed.): *Dialektičeskij materializm.* Moskva. 1954. Rozental', M. M., Štraks, G. M.: *Kategorii materialistíčeskoj dialektiki.* Moskva. 1956. Tugarinov, V. P.: *Sootnošenie ...* 1956. *Osnovy marksistskoj filosofii.* Moskva. 1958. *(Osnovy).* Exceptions to this are: Kedrov, B. M.: *O količestvennyx i kačestvennyx izmenenijax v prirode.* Moskva. 1946 (p. 132ff.). Tugarinov, V. P.: *Zakony* p. 134.
22. Engels, F.: *Anti-Djuring.* Moskva. 1950 (p. 34).
23. Rožin, V. P.: *Marksistsko-leninskaja dialektika kak filosofskaja nauka.* (Henceforward: *Dialektika*). Leningrad. 1957 (p. 30). See the parsimonious explanation in the "Large Soviet Encyclopedia": "A principle (from Lat. *principium* = axiom *(načalo),* basis *(osnova))* is the essential propositional point of departure of a theory, doctrine, science, etc.; the internal conviction of men; man's view of things *(vzgljad na vešči)".* BSE. (ed. 2. Moscow. 1955) 34, 529.
24. Rožin *Dialektika* p. 31.
25. *Ibid.* Here is to be found a short presentation of the theory of principles in which the usual regularities of the dialectic (1. Movement and development, 2. Inter-connection and mutual determination) are, for the first time, defined as "general principles". This is not the case in *Osnovy* (see pp. 10–30, especially 11 and 25; and 202ff.).
26. Kopnin, P. V.: *Ideja i ee rol' v poznanii.* VF 1959, 9, 53–64 (here p. 60).

REFERENCES

27. *Ibid.* The second section of this affirmation is directed against Tugarinov who explains, in his *Zakony*, that a scientific principle is not expressed in a law (judgement) but in a concept, and indicates – as opposed to a law (connection) – a quality of the thing (on p. 134f.).
28. Ovsjannikov, M. F.: *Filosofija Gegelja.* Moskva. 1959 (IV, 3: *Učenie o ponjatii.* pp. 133–151; especially p. 146ff.).
29. See Ojzerman, T. I.: *O materialističeskom rešenii vtoroj storony osnovnogo voprosa filosofii.* V MGU SEFP 1959, 3, 147–154 (here p. 147).
30. The article *"Ideja"* in the KFS (p. 186f.) restricts itself to repeating the systematically worthless references from Stalin's *"Voprosy leninizma"* (see: ed. 11. Moskva. 1939–1947. p. 546f.). There is no mention of Lenin's crude polemic against Bogdanov's "substitution-theory" or of his correction of Dietzgen's *"Incursions of a Socialist into the Domain of Epistemology"* (see: Lenin, V. I.: *Materializm i empiriokriticizm.* In: Soč. 14. Here: p. 214 and 232f.).
31. Kopnin *op. cit.* p. 61.
32. Aleksandrov *op. cit.* p. 89.
33. *Ibid.* p. 90. For completeness, here are the most important passages of the entry on "Law" *(zakon)* in the "Large Soviet Encyclopedia" – preference has been given to Leninist texts: "Law (in philosophy) is the general, essential, i.e. durable, self-repeating and necessary in the phenomena of the world. The laws of science are reflections of the objective processes which take place in nature and society, independent of the will of man. The recognition of the objective character of the laws of science is one of the basic principles of philosophical materialism which definitively refutes the fantasies of idealism. This latter denies the objective character of laws and presents them as products of reason, of supernatural ideas, of divine pre-destination, etc. (Aquinas, Hume, Kant, Hegel, the Machists, etc.)." (BSE 16, 368). According to Lenin, the basic idea which was common to Hume and Kant is the "denial of the objective regularity of nature and the derivation of this or that 'condition of experience', this or that principle, postulate or supposition from the subject, from human consciousness and not from nature" (Lenin, V. I.: Soč. 14, 153). The difference between Hume's view ("Sensation and experience tell us not the least thing about any kind of necessity") and the Kantian-Machist formula ("Man dictates the laws to nature") is a "secondary difference between two agnostics who are in basic agreement on the denial of the objective regularity of nature" (Lenin *op. cit.* p. 151; see also 145 and 149).

"In opposition to idealism, which makes common cause with fideism, materialism recognizes the objective regularity of nature and the approximately correct reflection of this regularity in the consciousness of man. .... Knowledge of a law means penetration to the essence of phenomena, discovery of the general essential traits which are objectively proper to the infinitely diverse phenomena and processes" (BSE 16, 368). "Ergo", Lenin concludes, "law and essence are both concepts, concepts of the same order, or, better, of the same power, which express a deepening of man's knowledge of the phenomena of the world, etc. ...." "The concept of law is one of the levels of human knowledge of the unity and connection, of the mutual dependence and of the totality of the world-process" (Lenin, V. I.: *Filosofskie tetradi.* Moskva. 1947. pp. 127 and 126).
34. *Osnovy* p. 202.
35. *Ibid.* p. 203 (footnote).
36. Marx, K.: *Kapital.* Moskva. 1955 (vol. III, p. 233).

37. See: Rozental'-Štraks (pp. 171–176), Tugarinov *Sootnošenie* 1956 (p. 113) and Rožin *Dialektika* (p. 9).
38. Rožin *Dialektika* p. 38.
39. "In our philosophic literature the necessary distinction and correlation of law and regularity are not sufficiently heeded. One acts as if there were no distinction between law and regularity. This is false." (Tugarinov *Sootnošenie* 1956 p. 114).
40. *Ibid.*
41. *Ibid.* p. 115f.
42. See: Lenin, V. I.: *Materializm i empiriokriticizm.* In: Soč. 14. p. 29.

ON CATEGORIES IN SOVIET PHILOSOPHY

A SURVEY

The theory of the "categories" of Dialectical and Historical Materialism has, in post-Stalinist Soviet philosophy, been the scene of a remarkable animation and expansion. In the discussions [1] of 1954–56, the adverse circumstances which had up to then impeded the development of a theory of categories were overcome and, from then on, the meaning of the term "category" was discussed in an ever-growing number of articles, the single categories, groups of categories or even whole systems thereof were exposed, and suggestions for the ordering of the categorial system in the architectonic of Dialectical Materialism were offered for discussion.

THE DEFINITION OF THE TERM "CATEGORY"

What Dialectical Materialism understands by "category" can be completely seen only from a consideration of its whole theory of categories. But the following provisional, nominal, definition can be found in the "Short Philosophic Dictionary": "Categories in philosophy are the basic logical concepts which reflect the most general and most essential qualities, aspects and relationships of the objects and phenomena of reality. The categories have arisen in the course of the historical development of knowledge on the basis of the material-productive, social practice of man. .... Knowledge is a complicated process of the formation of categories, concepts, laws." [2]

This means that the categories are conceptual and not – as in the thought of Hegel – "degrees of development of an absolute, mystico-religious idea", or elements of an ideal reality. Further, they do not form an *a priori*, closed system – as was Kant's view – but there is a historical process of formation and variation of the stock of categories: "Being reflections of the essential inter-connections of reality, the categories must necessarily be as mobile, elastic and inter-connected as are the objects and processes of the material world itself." Finally, it is stressed that the concrete is represented in its perfection not by isolated *(otdel'nye)* categories, which each reflect only a specific aspect of the world, but by the organic totality of the categories. This brings to mind Lenin's image with which he wished to make clear the sense of the categories: "Before man extends a net of natural phenomena. ... The categories are degrees of accentuation, ... the nodal points of the net, which help in knowing and gaining control over it."[3]

From this provisional definition it is immediately clear that Soviet philosophers understand the categories not only as devices of thinking but also as devices of an understanding thought which grasps its object – the categories have, therefore, an essentially ontological aspect and, despite its appellation of "dialectical logic"[4], the theory of categories belongs in the domain of ontology. Most of the contemporary investigations are devoted to the ontological aspect of the theory of categories.

THE MOST IMPORTANT WORKS ON CATEGORIES

The pronouncements on the nature and function of the categories, which we find in the special researches on the question, are marked by an immediately evident increase in precision and distinction over those of the "Short Philosophic Dictionary". But, before going into the question in detail, it seems in order that we become acquainted with those basic philosophic concepts which are designated as "categories".

The dictionary of Rozental' and Judin lists the following as "Categories of Dialectical Materialism": matter, motion, time, space, quality, quantity, inter-connection, contradiction, necessity (and chance), form and content, essence and appearance, possibility and actuality, "etc."[5]. Further, we find numerous basic categories of Historical Materialism listed, e.g., means of production, socio-economic formation, forces of production, base and superstructure, class, revolution, etc.[6]

In a collective work, edited by Rozental' and Štraks (1956),[7] on the categories of the materialist dialectic a group of categories (without any detailed analysis in the book itself) is named "by which are expressed the basic laws of the dialectic", i.e. quality, quantity, measure, contradiction, negation, etc.[8]. Rozental' indicates in his introduction that the special sciences also have their own specific categories – mass, matter, light, energy, atom, for physics; life, species, heredity, mutability, for biology [9]. The following categories or groups thereof were treated in detail in this book: phenomenon and essence, cause and effect, necessity and chance, law, content and form, possibility and actuality, singular, particular and universal, abstract and concrete, historical and logical.

A more comprehensive listing (and, at least partially, interpretation) of the categories is to be found in the works of V.P. Tugarinov, who, to our mind, is the most important of contemporary Soviet categoricians. His article on the inter-relationship of the categories of Dialectical Materialism (1956) and his book [10] of the same name develop a system of categories which are divided according to the traditional distinction between objects, qualities and relations. In the first group, the "categories of substance", we find: nature, being, matter, phenomenon; in the second, "attributive categories": motion, change, development, space, time, objective – subjective, consciousness – thought; the "relative" categories, which include inter-connection and relations, are: necessity – chance, content – form, causality – finality, possibility – actuality, universal – particular – singular [11]. Tugarinov's original analyses have found more of an echo among his contemporaries than those of any of his fellow categoricians.[12]

Shortly before Tugarinov's article on categories appeared, E. P. Sitkovskij proposed an extensive scheme for the systematic presentation of Dialectical Materialism as a "dialectico-logical" theory of categories [13]. In a surprisingly strict imitation of Hegel, he sketched a three-membered doctrine of *being*, of *essence*, of *concept* – naturally, in the direction of a materialist solution of the "basic question of philosophy", speaking neither of the being of an absolute idea nor of a neutral being, but of the being of material things [14]. The doctrine on *being* is threefold: under the title *"quality of things"*, we find the categories being, non-being, becoming; time, space, motion; finite – infinite: the title *"quantity of things"* includes number, dimension and degree *(stepen')* (of development), multiplicity, universality, quantitative infinity: the *"measure of things"* comprehends measure as unity of the qualitative and quantitative, the dialectic of quantitative-qualitative changes, gradual-ness and sudden-ness, and the nodal line of commensurability. The second step of Sitkovskij's dialectico-logical explanation of what is, is the doctrine of the *essence of things*. It, in its turn, is three-fold, proceeding from essence (essence – appearance, law, thing and relation, contradiction – identity, difference, essential difference, opposition – unity and conflict of oppositions), through phenomenon (relation *(otnošenie)*) of things (substance – accident, base – resultant, cause – effect, inner – outer, form – content, reciprocity), to actuality (possibility and actuality, necessity and chance, negation and negation of negation, progressive development, the process of development of nature as a whole). The third section of Dialectical Materialism, the doctrine on *concept*, is also designated as the doctrine of the forms and laws of thought and is not as exemplarily divided as the first two – only a few examples are given: reflection theory, the basic forms of logical thought (concept, judgement, conclusion, proof, method), truth, practice as criterion of truth [15].

All this is proposed by Sitkovskij – as we have repeated it here – in its general lines and not in detail. He, unlike Tugarinov, did not later provide a detailed realization of his plan and there did not seem to be any special response on the part of his colleagues [16].

The sketches of the systems made by Tugarinov and Sitkovskij show the lofty goals which some authors set for the dialectico-materialist theory of categories [17]. But most of the Soviet philosophers who deal with categories, rather than tending to build great systems, restrict themselves to analytic or exegetic treatment of single categories or of strictly limited groups thereof. For the most part, they devote themselves to the categorial concepts which we have already met in the bigger lists. More often than not their researches are not called investigations of categories – but this does not alter the fact that they are just this.

Matter and its forms of mobility are oft-repeated themes not only of popular presentations but also of "experimental" contributions to discussions [18]. The same is true of the "existential forms", space and time, and of the problem of finity and infinity [19]. There is, here and there, a definite tendency to specifically treat of the ontological characteristics of matter.

Inter-connection and the dynamic of development, central categories of the dialectic, also receive much attention. Of particular interest are the diverse discussions of the dialectical contradiction in all areas of reality, and the exegeses in reference to the problem of the quantitative-qualitative changes and to the negation-of-negation complex – in other words, the categorial problematic of the three "basic laws" of the dialectic [20].

To the determinative categories, which were also included in the systematic presentations (causality, law, necessity, possibility, chance, freedom), are added, in the course of special investigations, such particular problems as those of intention and intentionality, probability and statistical regularity [21].

There is now a tendency to stress, in addition to the traditional categories of the dynamic of development, the concepts which can be called the categories of the static. The categorial group "object, quality, relation" is currently the theme of discussions and the term "structure" plays an increasingly important role in philosophical disputes – the same is true of such expressions as situation *(sostojanie)*, order *(porjadok)*, etc. A few works are devoted to the relationship between simple and complex, and between whole and part [22].

CATEGORIES AND CONCEPTS

As the name indicates, the categories have a certain propositional function. It would be of interest to see how much more clearly Soviet philosophers currently interpret the propositional content of the categories of Diamat, than is the case in the dictionary definition of Rozental' and Judin.

The dictionary calls categories "logical concepts" in which certain characteristics of the object – the most "universal and essential" – are "reflected". Thus, the categorial concepts are simply designations of qualities, "sides" and relations. In reference to their epistemological nature, this tells us, at least, that they do not indicate concrete objects but abstract moments of different kinds. Thus, Rozental', who usually treats "concepts and categories" as synonyms, corrects himself in a footnote: "The words 'concept' and 'category' are usually treated as synonyms. But there is a certain difference between them. There are concepts which cannot be called categories, e.g. such simple concepts as table, horse, man, machine, instrument, etc." Rozental' then repeats his old dictionary definition [23]. In an entirely different perspective, D. P. Gorskij indicates a distinction between the "categories of the dialectic" and certain "very general concepts" which are used in formal logic, like "logical form", "logical consequence", "extension of the concept".[24] According to Gorskij such concepts are not categories of Dialectical Materialism because they contain an abstraction from the essential real relations (like time, process, development and change of the objects) and they take into account only the "logical form of thought", while the dialectic pays specific attention to the relationship to dynamic reality [25]. Further, Gorskij does not give any general ear-mark whereby categories could be distinguished from other general concepts – something along the line of specific or generic concepts, the designation of "properties" (like "red") or of activities, etc. Gorskij uses the term "universals" for the categories [26], but presumably not in the narrow sense which is found in the "Short Philosophic Dictionary" [27], i.e. as a specific or generic term *(vidovye, rodovye i obščie ponjatija)*. Tugarinov, who had interpreted categories as the "highest generic concepts of science" in an earlier work [28], does not hold this opinion in his later works. We find a general discussion on the nature of categories in an article on the categories of Historical Materialism by V. Ž. Kelle and M. Ja. Koval'zon. They maintain, too, that "not all concepts are categories". One catches a glimpse of a positive characterization of the categories in "The categories are the result of an analysis, of a dissection of the object . . ." [29].

In short, we can say that categories are concepts which indicate neither concrete objects nor genera nor collections, but reduction-products of different kinds, viz. abstract structure-moments or complexes of such structure-moments, exceptionally general and essential "qualities, aspects and relations". Tugarinov adds that there are categories which indicate the "general objects" *(obščie predmety)* or substrata [30].

CATEGORIES AND "BASIC LAWS"

In contemporary Soviet works on categories the question of the formal distinction of the categories from the other types of concepts is of much less importance than the question of the connections between the categories and the laws, specifically the "basic laws of the dialectic".

The allusion to the "general and essential qualities, aspects and relations" does not fully explain the propositional function of the categories. The basic form of the proposition – for Dialectical Materialism, too – is the judgement. Therefore, the question as to the relation of the categories to judgements and to laws (as a specific type of judgement) is of importance. A series of Soviet authors have dealt with this subject and the answers are not uniform.

The accepted version, which is, without a doubt, still the most wide-spread today, is presented by M. M. Rozental' as follows: knowledge is the discovery of laws; "But laws are known by means of concepts and categories". There are three basic laws of the dialectic which are expressed with the help of certain categories (quantity, quality, contradiction, negation, etc.), ". . . but they do not make up the whole of the dialectical theory of development. .... Categories of the materialist dialectic, like phenomenon and essence, cause and effect, necessity and chance, content and form, etc., complete the Marxist dialectical method with new notes and new aspects"[31].

D. P. Gorskij gave a similar presentation of the affair in his article which appeared before the book of Rozental' and Štraks: "It must be stressed ..., that all the categories of Dialectical Materialism play an essential role in the formulation of the laws of the Marxist dialectical method." Gorskij lists the three basic laws according to Engels and adds that the general, regular inter-connections which are reflected in the "categories" (essence – phenomenon, form – content, etc.) "through their very essence also represent laws of the dialectic", that the categories "fix" certain dialectical regularities in shortened form. Whence he draws the conclusion: "There is no difference of principle between the categories and laws of the dialectic", but only a "fine line" – the "main laws" of the dialectic are especially necessary for the characterization of development, while "the categories of the dialectic fill out and concretize the general conception of development ..."[32].

This sketchy and incommensurable data (the categories are both presupposed by and subordinated to the basic laws) called forth from other Soviet philosophers the cry of contradiction and efforts to get on the track through careful analyses of the meaning of the concepts. Important in this context are the articles of Tugarinov and Kelle-Koval'zon and, even more, Tugarinov's book of 1956 [33].

Tugarinov points out that Gorskij makes no clear distinction between concepts and judgements. The categories as more specific propositions are subsumed under the laws as more general propositions. This is not possible; furthermore, there are both basic laws *and* categories as well as non-basic (neosnovnye) laws and categories [34]. In the same line, Kelle and Koval'zon point out that Gorskij would allow only a slight difference between laws and categories and answer that, although one should not absolutise the difference between them, all the same, there is a difference and it is essential – the laws reflect essential, constant and recuring inter-connections of reality, while the categories reflect single "essential aspects or moments" of the same reality. Essential to an investigation of categories is that the "single sides of the object which are in question" be stressed and clearly set off from one another. "If there is no essential difference between the categories and

70

the laws of science – basically, categories are laws and laws categories – then a special investigation of categories has no sense."[35] Even more clearly is stressed in Tugarinov's book that the categories are presupposed in all the laws of the dialectic and materialism, and, therefore, are methodologically subordinate, in a certain sense, to these laws. "Every law of Dialectical Materialism is a correlation of categories."[36]
Further, the category, as a purely conceptual term, is not a judgement and, consequently, not a law. It is true that – like the bud the flower – it contains a series of judgements (laws)[37]. Tugarinov calls the provisional delimitation of an essential inter-connection "regularity" *(zakonomernost')* and reserves the term "law" *(zakon)* for the explicit formulation of specific, essential relations[38].
The text-books of 1958 and 1959[39] gave no final solution to the problem of how the categories are related to the "basic question" and to the "basic laws". Their authors avoided presenting the categories according to the schema of Rozental' and Gorskij (or even older models), as a sort of appendix to the three basic laws. Instead, some of them (inter-connection, cause – effect, law, essence, individual – particular – universal, necessity – chance, possibility – actuality) are quite sensibly put before the three chapters on the basic laws and the others (content – form, essence – phenomenon, and generalities on the categories as forms of knowing) are introduced at various places in the exegesis of the basic laws[40]. This provisional compromise-solution was accepted by some and criticised by others[41].

THE FUNCTION OF THE THEORY OF CATEGORIES
IN DIALECTICAL MATERIALISM

The revivification of the theory of categories is remarkable for several reasons. One can speak of its analytic and synthetic aspects[42]. It is a matter: (1) of once and for all very simply clarifying the meanings which are bound up with the categorial terms. This is the task of a logical analysis of meaning *(smyslovyj analiz)* of the categories – so to speak, a categorial semantic. It is V. P. Tugarinov who has most clearly formulated this task[43]. This is, without any question, the most pressing task which present-day Soviet philosophy has to solve and it is here that most of the work has been done up to now. (2) of finding the various ways in which the totality of the categories may be distributed. Various beginnings have been made in this direction but, on the whole, one has progressed not much farther than what might be called the "rhapsody" stage. A certain "regional" grouping has come into use – categories which are tied up with the "basic question"; categories on which the "basic laws" are founded; categories of Historical Materialism; and categories of the special sciences. Up to now the functional differences between ontological, epistemological, logical and methodological categories have hardly been investigated [44], and the same is true of the morphological differences between the substratal, attributive, relational, modal and determinational categories [45]. Somewhat more clearly defined are the conceptions of a "stratification" of the categories according to the lower and higher "modes of movement of matter".

For the synthetic aspect the first task is clarifying the internal connections between the categories. Such connections are expressed in the terms "coordination" and "subordination" and the goal of the effort is to provide a complete subordination-sequence for all categories. Different authors have gone after a workable "guide-line" for the construction of the system of categories and have come up with different variations on the Hegelian model [46]. But they are fully aware of the provisional character of such attempts [47]. "It would be naive to maintain that one could 'in passing' construct a 'complete course' of dialectical logic or, from only the most general considerations, *a priori* regulate its structure – following Hegel or anyone else – in such a way as to exclude any other approach. In the present stage of development, one must limit oneself to more moderate tasks – step by step to orient oneself on the nature, content and inter-connections of the categories . . . and postpone the inevitable objections until this preparatory work has produced results."[48]

Herewith is the last word said also on the second, synthetic, aspect of the theory of categories, i.e. on the architectonic problem of the best possible location of the theory of categories within the total system of Dialectical Materialism. This problem is of utmost significance since it foreshadows a profound revision of the current presentations of Dialectical Materialism but, at the moment, the time is not ripe to speak about it in Soviet philosophy. This is very clearly exemplified by the untoward manner in which, e.g., O. R. Gropp (Leipzig) intervened in the Soviet discussion [49].

One can only hope that Soviet philosophers will systematically proceed along the road indicated by V. P. Tugarinov. The eminently progressive significance of the revivified theory of categories consists in the fact that it seeks clarity and precision [50] in the domain of the basic philosophic concepts. It is precisely this which has been lacking in the past years and the progress which may be noted as of 1954 is still quite modest. The number of specialists who occupy themselves with the theory of categories is not too big and even these do not consider categories as the central problem of their investigations. Nevertheless, one can expect that further progress will have as its result that the theses of Dialectical Materialism will be increasingly better formulated, differentiated and supported and thereby become open to discussion, and that gradually many of the dogmatic blocks will be removed. This is why the new theory of categories in Soviet philosophy deserves a lively scientific interest[51].

REFERENCES

1. Reports in VF 1954, 3–5. "Kommunist" 1954, 13 and 14. Articles in VF 1955, 3 and 5; 1956, 1, 2 and 3. Report on the coordination conference in the IF AN SSSR (28 to 30 June 1956) in VF 1956, 6.
2. *Kratkij filosofskij slovar'*. (KFS) (ed. 4) 1955. pp. 186–187.
3. Lenin, V. I.: *Filosofskie tetrady*, p. 67. A short sketch of the Leninist theory of categories is to be found in Simuš, P. I.: *Nekotorye voprosy dialektiki v trude V. I. Lenina "Materializm i empiriokriticizm"*. FN 1959, 3, 34–44. A detailed exegesis is to be found in " *O 'Filosofskix tetradjax' V. I. Lenina"* (published by the AN BSSR, Moscow, 1959, 448 pp.) on pp. 132–202.
4. Because of the theses of Engels and Lenin on the identity of the laws of nature, society and thought and on the "coincidence" of the philosophical disciplines of dialectic, epistemology and logic, attempts at diversified treatment have up to now developed very slowly.
5. P. 186.
6. *Ibid.*
7. *Kategorii materialističeskoj dialektiki*. Moskva. 1956. 389str. German edition: *Kategorien der materialistischen Dialektik*. Berlin. 1959.
8. German edition p. 7.
9. *Ibid.* p. 15.
10. *Sootnošenie kategorii dialektičeskogo materializma*. VF 1956, 3, 151–160. *Sootnošenie kategorii dialektičeskogo materializma*. Leningrad. 1956. 122str.
11. Article p. 158; Book pp. 17–19.
12. Review by A. Gulyga in *"Deutsche Zeitschrift für Philosophie"* 1957, 5, 634–638. Criticised by Afanas'ev, V. G.: *O sootnošenii kategorii: vešč, svojstvo i otnošenie (zamečanija na knigu V. P. Tugarinova)*. VF 1958, 1, 179–181. The sharp rejection by Götz Redlow: *Materie oder Substanz?* in *"Philosophie im Klassenkampf"*. Berlin. 1959. (pp. 24–44) was shown to be insufficiently grounded by a Soviet reviewer (VF 1959 11, 183). Other controversies are indicated in VF 1959, 11, 162. See also the review of F. T. Arxipcev's book on matter in VF 1958, 10, 150–154. German literature on the question includes: Gropp, R. O.: *Zu Fragen der Geschichte der Philosophie und des dialektischen Materialismus*. Berlin. 1958. (pp. 117–128). Albrecht, E.: *Beiträge zur Erkenntnistheorie und das Verhältnis von Sprache und Denken*. Halle. 1959 (p. 226). Polikarov, A.: *Bemerkungen zu dem Artikel von Götz Redlow "Materie oder Substanz?"* in *"Deutsche Zeitschrift für Philosophie* 1960, 1–2, 169–171. These (incomplete) indications show that Tugarinov's theses provoked a discussion which those of others had not done.
13. *Lenin o sovpadenii v dialektičeskom materializme dialektiki, logiki i teorii poznanija*. in VF 1956, 2, pp. 77–90. German translation in "Sowjetwissenschaft. Gesellschaftswissenschaftliche Beiträge" 1956, 12.
14. *Ibid.* p. 85.
15. *Ibid.* pp. 85–87.
16. A complete and detailed criticism is given by O. R. Gropp in the above-mentioned (note 12) book. The section on the problem of the dialectico-materialist theory of categories appeared in revised form as *K voprosu o marksistskoj dialektičeskoj logike kak sisteme kategorij* in VF 1959, 1, 149–157.
17. V. S. Bibler's book *"O sisteme kategorij dialektičeskoj logiki"* (Stalinabad. 1958) has

74

not yet been evaluated. In addition to the works already mentioned, the following are general works on categories: Rožin, V. P., Podkorytov, G. A., Emdin, M. V.: *Kategorii dialektičeskogo materializma*. Leningrad. 1956. Pancxava, I. D.: *Material k lekcii na temu: "Kategorii materialističeskoj dialektiki"*. Moskva. 1957. Žegida, N. I.: *Osnovnye kategorii materialističeskoj dialektiki*. Voronež. 1958. Dmitriev, A. A.: *Osnovnye kategorii materialističeskoj dialektiki*. Moskva. 1958. *Kategorii materialističeskoj dialektiki*. Kiev. 1959 (in Ukrainian). Bortkevič, N. A.: *Osnovnye kategorii materialističeskoj dialektiki*. Moskva. 1959. The categories of *Historical* Materialism have, since 1956, been mentioned in several works: Kelle, V. Ž., Koval'zon, M. Ja.: *Kategorii istoričeskogo materializma*. VF 1956, 4. Čagin, V. A., Xarčev, A. G.: *O kategorijax "proizvoditel'nye sily" i "proizvodstvennye otnošenija"*. VF 1958, 2. Tugarinov, V. P.: *O kategorijax "obščestvennoe bytie" i "obščestvennoe soznanie"*. VF 1958, 1. To which we find a critical reply: Glezerman, G. E.: *K voprosu o ponjatii "obščestvennoe bytie"*. VF 1958, 5. Tugarinov, V. P.: *Sootnošenie kategorij istoričeskogo materializma*. Leningrad. 1958. (extract in an article: *O sootnošenii kategorij istoričeskogo materializma*. FN 1959, 1.) *Kategorii istoričeskogo materializma*. (pod. red. M. Džunusova). Frunze. 1959. With the exception of the last three, these works have appeared in German translation in "Sowjetwissenschaft. Gesellschaftswissenschaftliche Beiträge'".

18. Arxipcev, F. T.: *V. I. Lenin o naučnom ponjatii materii*. Moskva. 1957. and *Ponjatie materii i osnovnoj vopros filosofii*. VF 1958. 12. The review of Arxipcev's book by E. G. Gendel' (VF 1958, 10) contains further references to literature on the discussion of the concept of matter. M. N. Rutkevič added some new elements to the discussion of the forms of motion of matter in *K voprosu o klassifikacii form dviženija materii* in FN 1958, 1, 77–89.

19. On space and time: Sviderskij, V. I.: *Prostranstvo i vremja. Filosofskij očerk*. Moskva. 1958. Meljuxin, C. T.: *Problema konečnogo i beskonečnogo. Filos. očerk*. Moskva. 1959. See also the extensive discussion on matter, space and time, in the frame of the "Philosophy of the Natural Sciences."

20. General works on the basic laws and categories: Rozental'-Štraks: *Kategorii materialističeskoj dialektiki* (see note 7). Andreev, I. D.: *Osnovnye zakony i kategorii materialističeskoj dialektiki*. Moskva. 1959. Pancxava, I. D.: *Dialektičeskij materializm*. Moskva. 1958. V. P. Rožin's book *"Marksistsko-leninskaja dialektika kak filosofskaja nauka"* (Leningrad. 1957) met heavy opposition (see FN 1958, 3). The articles by Gorskij, Kelle-Koval'zon and Tugarinov are cited below. Indications of literature on the discussions on contradictions, quantitative and qualitative changes, and on the negation of negation (there are over 40 titles for this last) are out of place here. But, M. N. Rutkevič's article *"O suščnosti zakona otricanija otricanija i sfere ego dejstvija"* (FN 1958, 4) should be mentioned because it deals with important aspects of the over-all conception of development.

21. Anissimov, S. F.: *Sootnošenie kategorij zakona, pričinnosti neobxodimosti i slučajnosti*. VF 1955, 6. Jaxot, O. O.: *Neobxodimost' i slučajnost'*. Moskva. 1956. Dubrovskij, D. I.: *K voprosu ob opredelenii kategorii slučajnosti*. VF 1957, 3. Fedorov, G. A.: *Materialisticeskaja dialektika o kategorii celi*. VF 1956, 1. Makarov, M. G.: *K istorii kategorii "cel'" v domarksovoj filosofii*. VF 1959, 10. Frolov, I. T.: *Determinizm i teleologija*. VF 1958, 2. Rubinštejn, S. L.: *Voprosy psixologii myšlenija i princip determinizma*. VF 1958, 12. Smirnov, L. V.: *Kategorija verojatnosti*. VF 1958, 12. Jaxot, O. O.: *Determinizm i statistika*. VF 1958, 10. Tugarinov, V. P.: *Zakony ob'ektivnogo mira, ix poznanie i ispol'zovanie*. Leningrad. 1954. and *Zakony prirody i obščestva*.

REFERENCES

Moskva. 1957. Kovalgin, V. M.: *Dialektičeskij materializm o zakonax nauki.* Minsk. 1958. Tulenov, Ž.: *Zakon kak filosofskaja kategorija.* Alma-Ata. 1959.

22. Tugarinov, V. P.: *O kategorijax predmeta, svojstva i otnošenija.* Izv. LGU 1956, 17. and *Sootnošenie kategorij dialektičeskogo materializma.* Leningrad. 1956. Novik, I. B.: *O kategorijax "vešč'" i "otnošenie".* VF 1957, 4. Man'kovskij, L. A.: *Kategorii "vešč'" i "otnošenie" v "Kapitale"* K. Marksa. VF 1956, 5. Afanas'ev, V. G.: *O sootnošenii kategorij: vešč', svojstvo i otnošenie.* VF 1958, 1. Blauberg, I. V.: *O kategorijax celogo i časti v marksistskoj filosofii.* VF 1957, 4. Afanas'ev, V. G.: *O kategorijax prostogo i složnogo.* VF 1956, 1. Kristostur'jan, N. G.: *O sootnošenii obščego i otdel'-nogo v poznanii.* VF 1954, 6. Grušin, B. A.: *Marks i sovremennye metody istoričeskogo issledovanija.* VF 1958, 3. Kedrov, B. M.: *O dialektiko-logičeskom obobščenii istorii estestvoznanija.* VF 1960, 1. Remarks on the relation of universal, particular and individual and abstract and concrete are favourite themes of the last few years. A quite important work on the category "inter-connection" is Uemov, A. I.: *O dialektiko-materialističeskom ponimanii svjazi meždu javlenijami.* FN 1958, 1. Noteworthy on "form-content" is: Man'kovskij, L. A.: *Kategorija formy i ee aspekty (iz logičeskix kommentariev k "Kapitalu"* K. Marksa). FN 1958, 3. and Garkavenko, F. I.: *O roli formy v razvitii.* FN 1959, 1.

23. German edition p. 15f.

24. *O kategorijax materialističeskoj dialektiki.* VF 1955, 3. German translation in "Sowjetwissenschaft. Gesellschaftswissenschaftliche Beiträge" 1955, 6 and in a pamphlet *"Über die Kategorien der materialistischen Dialektik".* Berlin. 1956 (pp. 3–31). Other authors speak of special "logical categories".

25. *Ibid.* pp. 20–21.

26. *Ibid.* p. 20.

27. *Ibid.* p. 496.

28. *Zakony ob'ektivnogo mira, ix poznanie i ispol'zovanie.* Leningrad. 1954 (p. 97).

29. Kelle, V. Ž., Koval'zon, M. Ja.: *Kategorii istoričeskogo materializma.* VF 1956, 4. German translation in "Sowjetwissenschaft. Gesellschaftswissenschaftliche Beiträge" 1957, 1 and in the collective work *"Philosophie und Gesellschaft".* Berlin. 1958 (pp. 449–472).

30. VF 1956, 3, 152.

31. German edition p. 7.

32. *Ibid.* pp. 18–20.

33. Tugarinov: *Sootnošenie* pp. 112–115.

34. VF 1956, 3, 152–154.

35. German text in "Sowjetwissenschaft. ..." 1957, 1 (p. 41).

36. *Ibid.* p. 112.

37. VF 1956, 3, 152.

38. *Sootnošenie* p. 114; *Zakony* p. 35, 132f.

39. *Osnovy marksistskoj filosofii.* 1958. Iz. 2 1959. *Osnovy marksizma-leninizma.* Moskva. 1959.

40. *Osnovy marksistskoj filosofii.* 1959 (pp. 186–217: *Zakonomernaja svjaz' javlenij dejstvitel'nosti*) and (pp. 313–320: *Formy myšlenija i ix rol' v poznanii*), etc.

41. Reports on the discussions in VF 1959, 4, 115–119; VF 1959, 7, 160–165; FN 1959, 1, 238–241.

42. Thus Tugarinov in VF 1956, 3, 160.

43. *Sootnošenie* pp. 21–22.

44. A significant start in this direction has been made by V. V. Stoljarov in *"Über die*

Rolle und Stellung der philosophischen Kategorien im Denken" in "Deutsche Zeit-schrift für Philosophie" 1957, 5 (pp. 672–696). Tugarinov in VF 1956, 3, 160, *"problema kategorij – eto ne 'čisto' logičeskaja, no odnovremenno i ontologičeskaja, i gnoseologičeskaja i metodologičeskaja problema"*. See Gropp in VF 1959, 1.

45. As far as we have seen, only Tugarinov can be named in this context. In addition to his triple division, he has also grouped the categories in smaller sets or "nests".

46. The name of such investigations is the categorial pair "logical and historical". It plays an important part in the works of Rozental' ("Kommunist" 1956, 7), Sitkovs-kij, Tugarinov and others. The historical guide-line for the construction of the system is one time the history of philosophy and science (the appearance of the categories in thought) and the other the supposed sequence of the construction of the real world itself.

47. So, too, Rozental': "The problem of the system of categories, of the place of each category in this system, is a very essential problem and one which has not yet been elaborated in our literature." (*Kategorien der materialistischen Dialektik*. p. 55).

48. Tugarinov: *Sootnošenie* p. 21.

49. *"Zu Fragen der Geschichte der Philosophie und des dialektischen Materialismus"*. Ber-lin. 1958. The section which interests us appeared as contribution to a discussion (see notes 12 and 16). We hold the criticism of Sitkovskij's exaggeratedly Hegelian thesis on the identity of the logical and historical to be justified, but his criticism of the conception of category misses the point completely. The reason for this is simply that he knew Tugarinov only through Gulyga's review and was not able to grasp his "dialectical" conception of the relationship between categories, judgements and laws (or theories) (see the footnote in the book pp. 119–120; in VF 1959, 1, 151–152).

50. It seems that Descartes' *"claire et distincte"* has had some influence on Tugarinov's development: "It was R. Descartes who said: 'Define the meaning of words and you will free the world from half of its errors.'" *(Sootnošenie* p. 19).

51. A careful differentiation of the conceptual apparatus would profit not only profes-sional philosophy but also political ideology. But the real meaning of the theory of categories lies more in the area of pure science.

EINSTEIN AND SOVIET PHILOSOPHY *

INTRODUCTION

Since 1950 a discussion on the truth and foundations of the theory of relativity has been carried on in Soviet science. It resulted in a complete rejection of the theory by the Party philosophers, which was followed by an equally radical recognition in 1955. Since then the discussion has been carried on on an ever rising philosophical and scientific level and aims at the clarification of precise questions which are the object of discussion even in the West, as can be seen from Schilpp's "Einstein – Philosopher and Scientist" (1949). Our goal is primarily a historical presentation of the points of view expressed in the USSR in the relevant conferences, publications and Party decrees.

From this documentary foreground can be distinguished the more profound and purely philosophical struggle for the mastery of contemporary physics. Even though the problems involved are often expressed in a naive and even completely primitive form in the USSR, it cannot be denied that the traditional basic concerns of philosophical thought are touched on. This phenomenon is all the more remarkable in view of the fact that Soviet philosophy opposes the positivism of contemporary "philosophy of science" with a radical objectivism whereby it falls back, as far as its attitude is concerned, to pre-Kantian rationalism and even to the pre-Socratics with their question on the last and sole foundation of being. For some, such an undertaking in the middle of the 20th century might seem to be an anachronism; for others, an old-fashioned and complete misunderstanding of philosophical concerns; finally, others feel themselves repelled by the oft-repeated and richly emotional "proofs" of Soviet philosophers. Nevertheless, there is no doubt that Soviet philosophy's elementary impulse

---

* Because of the great complexity of the subject matter, the author thought it better not to burden this article with a disproportionate number of notes. Full references to sources are to be found in: Müller-Markus, S.: *Einstein und die Sowjetphilosophie. Krisis einer Lehre. I.* (Sovietica, Abhandlungen 1). Dordrecht. 1960.

toward a break-through of thought to reality is an expression of the philosophic movement toward the transcendent – which began already with Husserl and N. Hartmann.

Behind the Soviet struggle to think out the theory of relativity is, in the final analysis, a search for a new metaphysical mastery of nature. In view of the significant rise in level in Soviet philosophy as of 1955, and in view of the introduction of obligatory courses in natural science for students of philosophy, it seems that the future holds many surprises in this respect. Therefore, the Western reader should not let himself be deceived by the ever-present Soviet efforts to force the data of physics in a stereotyped way into the procrustean bed of Diamat. Such efforts are characteristic of an ever-receding, reactionary wing of Soviet philosophy. First-rate physicists like Fok, Ivanenko, A. D. Aleksandrov, etc., have long ago set out on their own road, which is much closer to a real ontology than to the antiquated doctrine of Engels and Lenin. The most important event in this context is Aleksandrov's attempt at the All-Union Conference (1958) to develop an "objectivist" deduction of the special theory of relativity.

Thus, the Western reader can certainly gain valuable insights into the problematic of the bases of contemporary physics from the Soviet discussion and can find suggestions which will aid his own understanding. Only through the common striving of all truth seekers the world over can be found the extremely difficult road through the no man's land of the unknown to a more exact metaphysics of nature.

THE EPISTEMOLOGICAL PROBLEMATIC

As first point the Soviet discussion took up the question of the epistemological aspect of the theory of relativity and the relevant attitude of its creator. According to the Soviets, Einstein was a partisan of all types of non-realist attitudes such as subjective idealism, conventionalism, operationalism, positivism and even solipsism. On the other hand, Einstein was a "materialist", i.e. realist. Such heterogeneous accusations force us to an examination of Einstein's epistemology as contained in his works. And it seems that Einstein's attitude is quite complex and cannot be easily classified. Nevertheless, the dominating note is a trust in the knowability of the physical world with the aid of a type of "pre-established harmony" between an axiomatically constructed, mathematical ideal-world and the

79

structure of reality. It is evident that the accusation of positivism which is brought against him is exaggerated, even though the demand of a principle of verification for the definition of physical concepts remains fully valid for him.

The Soviet philosophers have numerous objections to Einstein's method of presenting his theory. They have in mind a "materialist", i.e. an extreme empiricist, interpretation. Thus, the only motive of the physicist is industrial practicality; concepts are nothing but abstractions from the contents of experience; even the totality of mathematics is only abstraction plus a few dialectical inmixtures of the intellect. The purely rational, viz. constructive-axiomatic, origin of geometry or of the definition of the concept is rejected with vigour. This is especially true of "simultaneity" which is not to be defined with the help of natural laws but abstracted from the real world. Therefore, Soviet philosophers speak of "concrete" simultaneity. Further, the taking of the possibility of measurement as basic in the determination of the concept of simultaneity is rejected as leading to its relativization. Finally, the reduction of certain basic concepts of Diamat such as "absolute space", "matter", "motion", etc., to strict experience is rejected as contrary to materialism – whereby Diamat comes to light as a pseudo-metaphysics. In reference to the truth-value of concepts and theories, the ability to be reflected is postulated of physical reality and Einstein is reproached for having, through his demand for the axiomatic construction of concepts and theories, denied their truth-value. The criterion of truth to be preferred is not Einstein's simplicity of the logical bases and mathematical covariance but solely practice, which means industrial and, in the final analysis, partisan political, usefulness.

It can easily be shown that all the known methods of thought are used in the construction of the theory of relativity, and in such a way that they are difficult to separate. Most prominent, however, are the axiomatic and reductive. Methodologically, one can compare the theory to an axiomatic system whose axis freely rotates, on the one hand, in the construction of physical concepts and, on the other, in the reductive verification of conclusions. Beginning with the "zero-language" of the data of observation, passing through ever higher levels by conceptual construction and algebraic and geometric formalization, viz. language-formation, and arriving at the metalanguage of philosophic discussion, one elaborates a multilevel linguistic construction of the totality of the theory. Thereby, within the linguistic levels, there is a coordination such that the relations between the elements of one system correspond to quite an extent with those of the other system (as long as no new elements have been introduced) – thus, there is a thoroughly isomorphic correlation between the levels. In this way the conclusions from premises in the realm of the data of observation can be read from the conclusions in the geometrical realm of a system of coordinates and in the algebraic realm of vector and tensor analysis.

That which Einstein calls the "incomprehensible" consists in the fact that even the "zero-language" of the data of observation, i.e. the extremity of our conceptual bridge to nature, follows this law of isomorphic correlation, in spite of the fact that the meta-languages of the algebraic and geometric type can be constructed in a purely axiomatic way, by free postulation. This is one of the major problems of philosophy in general.

Diamat has not even been able to state the facts of the case, let alone explain them. For it, all meta-languages are but abstract images of natural facts. Further, there is no mention of the dialectical relationship of the elements of the various language-levels among themselves and in reference to neighbouring levels. Modern physics does not use the dialectical method which Diamat declares to be indispensable for science. Thus, already on methodological ground Diamat's claim of leadership in the natural sciences collapses.

THE SCIENTIFIC BASES OF THE SPECIAL THEORY OF RELATIVITY

The special theory of relativity is based on two principles: (1) the laws of nature are valid for all bodies moving uniformly in a straight line (relativity principle); (2) The speed of light remains constant for bodies moving uniformly in a straight line. From the relativity of the spatial and temporal intervals of events, follows the non-existence of absolute space (or its synonym, absolute ether), absolute time and absolute motion.

Soviet philosophy opposes these presuppositions of the theory with the radical thesis: from principles, no physical conclusions can be inferred – this means that *a priori* postulates have nothing more to do with experience. The speed of light varies from place to place – the relativity principle cannot be verified but remains always threatened with falsification (Jánossy).

To this it can be objected that the evaluation of a datum of observation as relevant to a theory of physics already presupposes the use of principles

81

of physics, the consequences of which alone can be used for confrontation. There is no theory without presupposed principles. The experiments of physics speak, without exception, for the relativity principle even though one must speak not of strict proof but more of approximation. Einstein maintained the speed of light as absolute only for the special theory of relativity and not for the broader instances where there were deviations from the inertial motion. Nevertheless, the Soviet references to the constant experimental danger both to the general principles and to the special relativity theory itself are methodologically valuable since they bring into relief the difficulties of theoretical physics. The principles of natural science cannot be established as valid – neither by induction, nor *a priori*, nor axiomatically – with any finality and the physicist must, in the final analysis, depend on a trust that real events are permeated by principles in general and by these principles in particular. Physics is always an adventure of knowledge.

The Soviet accusation that the relativity principle implies a philosophical relativity must be rejected. This accusation is based on a confusion of the several meanings of the same word. The relativity principle, as Fok and Aleksandrov correctly pointed out, is, on the contrary, based on the absolute character of the laws of nature (in distinction to inertial motion) and has nothing to do with philosophical relativity in the sense of an absolute equality of all points of view. This error can be traced back to certain positivist interpretations of the theory. When certain physical quantities such as length, duration, simultaneity and mass depend on a selected observation-post in an inertial system, then these quantities will, as a matter of fact, be relative (i.e. they will vary from one system of coordinates to another according to the Lorentz-transformation), but even these "relatively known" quantities are completely independent of the knower; otherwise, they could not be the objects of measurement. They are, then, as relative as they are objective. This relativity of the objective and objectivity of the relative is, according to the progressive section of Soviet philosophy, precisely the novelty introduced by the theory of relativity. Herein only the choice of the system of coordinates is left open since all inertial systems are, according to the relativity principle, completely equal; but once an observation-post has been selected, the measured quantities follow with necessity.

Some Soviet philosophers try to interpret the matter dialectically and thus build it into Diamat. In this sense Bazarov and others speak of the dialectical relation of the absolute to the relative. According to them, the absolute is the sum of all relative movements and paths as well as of all the relative extensions of bodies. There is, therefore, an absolute space which is the sum of relative spaces and an absolute motion which is the sum of all relative motion. Physics has nothing to do with such absolute spaces of the special theory of relativity. But it would seem, from Diamat's point of view, more consequent to admit as absolute only one single path of bodies, one single motion and, consequently, one single system of coordinates. Strangely enough, this thesis, which is absurd from the point of view of the theory of relativity, is espoused not only by the reactionaries (Maksimov, etc.), but even by Bloxincev, the director of the Central Institute for Atomic Research in Dubna. In opposition to this, Fok, Tamm and others appeal to the facts. The most recent interpretation is that of A. D. Aleksandrov (as of 1957), according to which there are, in fact, only relative motions but these are precisely the absolute fact which cannot be altered by any transformation of coordinates (change of observation-post); this is the dialectical relationship of "absolute" and "relative" which only Diamat is in a postion to solve. To this it can be objected that the terms "relative" and "absolute" are not used in the same regard and so there can be no question of a genuine contradictory relationship.

THE RELATIVITY OF "QUALITIES"

For Diamat, matter is a real substance in the sense of Descartes. It is being *per se* and *a se* – Spinoza's *causa sui* – endowed with the attributes, self-movement (within its existential forms – space and time), mass and extension. But the relativity principle renders impossible the acceptance of an absolute inertial motion and, thus, of an absolute system of coordinates for such motion. As a consequence, the attributes mass and extension are also dependent on the stand-point. It is senseless in physics to speak of the "mass-in-itself" and the "length-in-itself" of a body. And it is problematic whether one can speak of matter as substance in the above sense. As a result, Soviet philosophers made a special opposition to the relativity of "qualities". While the reactionaries under Maksimov tried to explain relativity as nothing but a fictive consequence of a modification of the scale of measurement and, thus, simply denied it, the other group under I.V. Kuznecov and Štejnman tried to explain relativity by recourse to the pre-

83

relativity interpretation of Lorentz – an interpretation which had already been shown to be false. In this version, the mass of a charged particle in motion increases because of structural changes in the field set up by itself (theory of electromagnetic mass). Just so the other effects (contraction of length and dilation of time) result from the field-effect which is the result of the relative motion of a body. Thus, the life-span of a particle of cosmic radiation increases in the field of the earth, but not as a simple result of its motion relative to the earth. From this it follows that all relativistic changes of qualities of moving bodies cannot be reduced to the relative velocity alone (more exactly to v^2/c^2) but rather to the real internal changes which take place in the moving bodies as a result of the structural changes of the fields of which these bodies are parts.

Soviet physicists discussed this "theory" at the Conference in Kiev (1954). Not one of them supported it. Rozencvejg called it "miserable trash"; others quite rightly pointed out its complete inadequacy for physics: if the effects were results of changes of field then they would have to diminish – as is the case with gravitation and the coulomb-transformations – according to the inverse square of the distance, which is evidently not the case. In addition, this conception denies relativity properly so-called, since only the motion in a once and for all, selected system of coordinates, that of the field (e.g. the field of the earth for cosmic radiations) causes the effect, while the relativity principle is based on indifference to all inertial systems.

It was openly stated in Kiev that official recognition of the "theory" of Štejnman-Kuznecov as the sole which agreed with Diamat would discredit Diamat itself.

As a result of this discussion the Party philosophy did a complete about-face in 1955. In January of that year the theory of relativity was officially recognized and the interpretation of the reactionaries was condemned as "subjectivist". Their leader, the Academician Maksimov, was removed from the editorial staff of *Voprosy filosofii*.

For all this, Soviet philosophy did not succeed in posing the real philosophic problem but only postponed it by recognizing the theory. The most progressive wing, under Fok and Aleksandrov, took pains to clarify the situation. According to them, the effects depended on the structure of space and time. Basic to the special theory of relativity is quasi-Euclidean, four-dimensional space-time, whose most important qualities are isotrophy, continuity and homogeneity. Therefrom follows mathematically the

Lorentz-transformation for length and simultaneity and, with it, all the effects of the theory.

I. V. Kuznecov drew, in Kiev, the consequences for Diamat when he said that this conception makes of the existential forms of matter (space and time) in reality, Aristotelian "forms" which have an active, formative role to play in connection with passive matter. But the solution to the problem seems to be not the interpretation of Kuznecov but rather the following: space and time are relational structures of a special sort without which physical entities cannot work on each other. All physical activities make the transition from point of origin to their end-point with the help of fields of force. But, as the Michelson experiment of 1887 showed, fields have no substratum such as ether. They are, obviously, an as yet not completely explained (philosophically, at least) something which, in any case, is not the cause of the relativity effects. Their cause is the structure of the spatio-temporal relations of bodies as developed by Fok and Aleksandrov. This structure is fixed, before any activity between bodies. In distinction to the version of Kuznecov-Štejnman, the cause of the relativity effects is not a force but a relational structure which, in its turn, determines the disposition of possible activities between bodies. The special theory of relativity leads that dynamic causality which had previously been taken as the only to be considered real in physics, to a structural causality. This, in its turn, because of the limitation of the propagation of light and of any propagation of activity, leads with conceptual necessity to the structure of a succession of events which are connected by real activity, and thus to classical causality. Aleksandrov recognized this fact in 1958.

The conclusion to be drawn from this reads: the physical event is directly determined not only by activities but also by the spatio-temporal structure of the part of the world in which it is. Structures, however, do not belong to the existential level of physically active factors – they are not experimentally measured, but are inferred from the measurements in a purely rational way. They are, therefore, intelligible entities of a rational sort and origin, typical of rational entities *cum fundamento in re*. As a consequence, the theory of relativity becomes a "protophysical" theory which structurally establishes physical activity. This immediately excludes from the realm of physics any type of materialism, i.e. any type of monism which recognizes only the physical substratum – and not the ordering of events – as irreducible constituent of the real world.

MASS AND ENERGY

While a materialist or physical monism is excluded by the relativity of "qualities", it is put seriously in question by the relationship $E = mc^2$. Here, to every mass corresponds an energy-value and vice versa. According to this law, material particles are transformed into vibratory energy and this into particles. Even though the Leninist definition of matter refers only to its independence from consciousness, a tendency in Soviet philosophy and physics (including Maksimov, Ioffe and many others) was officially condemned in 1951 for wanting to take energy as the unique substance of the world. Thereby, Diamat's purely epistemological concept of matter is reduced to the ontological concept of pre-Marxian materialism.

Unavoidably one meets the ontological problem of whether or not one can, as Diamat maintains, before and after (the above change) accept mass as the unique substance of the world. Up to the present, Soviet philosophy has defended the law of the conservation of mass, which was rendered obsolete by the theory of relativity, and denies the transformation of mass into energy. Energy is held more to be a form of the motion of matter which, as bearer of the motion, cannot change its form (Ovčinnikov, Suvorov, and others).

This subject was taken up in a conference in the Institute of Philosophy in Moscow and in a forum of the journal of theoretical physics (*Uspexi fizičeskix nauk*). The reactionary philosophers objected that the new conservation-propositions of the theory of relativity confuse the independent law of the conservation of mass with the law of energy. Terleckij stressed that, on the basis of the theory, one cannot even speak of a law of the conservation of matter. Nevertheless, the "energism" of the Soviet physicists was officially condemned.

But the physicists were not satisfied with this. Their most prominent spokesmen (Fok, Friš, Špol'skij) took a stand on the problem. In Fok's version, mass is related to energy as inertial-mass to gravitation-mass, both are numerically equivalent in certain conversion-formulae and both belong to the same entity. The difference between mass and energy is simply a matter of habit. In the majority of transformations of energy the mass of the system remains constant since it does not take part in the energy-process, or its participation therein is incommensurably small. The situation is different in the case of nuclear changes and radiation processes. Here, "passive mass = passive energy" is changed to "active mass = energy". Fok has not yet explained the physical basis for the non-participation of mass in the general instances of the transformation of energy. Within the limits of the general theory of relativity Fok comes to the conclusion that not only mass as a component of the energy-impulse vector but also every form of energy, participates in the determination of the spatio-temporal yardstick. Even here, mass appears as nothing but a form of energy distinct from space and time.

These lines of thought could be further developed, but it seems that the categorical identification of mass and energy must be rejected. If it were true, then one could be immediately reduced to the other. In spite of this, the formulae of theoretical physics, after as before (the theory), contain both. This is due to the fact that there is a difference between the reactions of the two factors. Potential energy is the "ability-to-come-about" of a configuration of events (of a physical system) – the actualization of these is kinetic energy or electromagnetic energy. Energy itself, then, exhibits the character of both existential modes, act and potency. It is for this very reason that any actualist monism such as that of Ostwald cannot be proposed on the basis of the propositions dealing with energy. In itself, then, energy follows mass as an "ability-to-come-about" of the second order, which can manifest itself in corresponding configurations of events of an actual thermal or electromagnetic, etc., character. Energy can be compared to capital which serves as reserve capable of realization; as circulating convertible currency representing a mass of accomplished, economically useful work; and as the "substance" of all economic bartering, participating as the scale of value in all work actually carried out.

Therefore, energy is a scale of the event and its possibility, but it is not the physical event itself. It is as little a world-substance as gold is the "substance" of human activity. The question as to the substance of events is, therefore, not solved and cannot be solved by a recourse to energy. Its clarification is a matter not for physics but for metaphysics.

THE DEVELOPMENT OF PHILOSOPHY AND
MARXISM-LENINISM IN POLAND
SINCE THE WAR[1]

The last sixty years have perhaps constituted the most remarkable period in the history of philosophy in Poland. Never before were so many talents and abilities attracted to philosophy, to make valuable contributions toward its development. Poland, after the First World War, having regained its own statehood and organised its institutions of teaching and research, became one of the important centres of philosophical inquiry [2]. Polish logicians (L. Chwistek, S. Leśniewski, J. Łukasiewicz, A. Tarski) and philosophers (K. Ajdukiewicz, T. Czeżowski, T. Kotarbiński, Z. Zawirski) promoted new trends and opened fresh fields of research. They reared the second generation of logicians and philosophers, who have continued the tradition established by the founders of the Warsaw school. Among those internationally known are the logicians, J. M. Bocheński, A. Grzegorczyk, S. Jaśkowski, A. Lindenbaum [3], J. Łoś, A. Mostowski, H. Rasiowa, J. Słupecki, B. Sobociński, M. Wajsberg [3], and the philosophers, J. Hosiasson [3], M. Kokoszyńska, J. Kotarbińska, H. Mehlberg, M. Ossowska and S. Ossowski [4].

Philosophy suffered grievous losses in human lives and research facilities during the German occupation. But the end of the hostilities of the Second World War [5] was followed by an outburst of creative intellectual energy. Mathematical logic at once resumed its former place in the international world of learning. At the International Congress of Philosophy in Amsterdam (1948) Polish philosophers did not turn up in person, but their contributions were numerous and of the same quality as in the past. Important works were published. Among the most outstanding were "Mathematical Logic" by Mostowski, "Logic" by Czeżowski, "The Foundations of the Science of Morals" and "Human Motivation" by Ossowska, "Philosophy of the Nineteenth Century and Contemporary Philosophy" by Tatarkiewicz, and "The Controversy over the Existence of the World" by Ingarden [6]. By the side of the two older generations of philosophers there appeared the younger one, which made a promising start. There was no reason to feel apprehensive that the present would not equal and even improve upon the past.

Just then, however, the course of development was again interrupted by political interference, suppression of free thought and speech, and the imposition of an oracular philosophy, enforced by administrative measures. The protracted struggle for the rights of reason, intellectual integrity, respect for facts, even the validity of logical thinking, began in earnest. The struggle was desperate, philosophical thinking appeared to be doomed. Then, in October 1956, came another upheaval. In its wake the submerged determination to search for truth and abide by its verdict has re-asserted itself with renewed strength.

Thus, there are three distinct periods in philosophical development in Poland after the Second World War. The first was the period of reconstruction which ended some time in 1949. It was marked by the rise of Marxism-Leninism as one philosophical trend among others which existed at that time in academic philosophy. Marxism-Leninism as a philosophical doctrine had a handful of supporters mostly outside the universities. They were regarded rather as philosophical and sociological journalists than professional philosophers. In their activities they tried to dispel what they called "the misrepresentations of Marxism-Leninism" and the wide-spread intellectual distrust of this doctrine, regarded as obsolete and wildly speculative and suspected of serving purely political aims under the guise of ostensible theoretical interests. For their part, Marxist-Leninists showed moderation in their publications concerning more specifically philosophical problems, kept on the defensive and adopted a conciliatory attitude toward other schools of thought with the exception of Christian philosophy.

While emphasizing their distinctive characteristics, Marxist-Leninists also professed themselves to be the inheritors and supporters of the rationalist and scientific tradition in philosophy. They spoke highly of the Warsaw school and logical empiricism, and indicated, at least verbally, their willingness to apply modern logical, syntactical and semantic methods to Marxist-Leninist theories. Philosophical discussions were outspoken and free; in the conditions of freedom of thought and expression, the Marxist-Leninist claim of having a philosophy superior to any other and of being in possession of the whole truth could have neither been made nor substantiated. The contrast between what Marxist-Leninist and non-Marxist philosophy had to offer was striking, to the informed and uninformed reader alike, and the contrast was not in favour of the Marxist-Leninists.

References pp. 98–99   89

Toward the end of 1947 the scientists and scholars on the one hand and the Marxist-Leninist circles on the other lived in a water-tight isolation. The former, Ossowski explained, considered Marxism-Leninism as "journalism which did not deserve serious consideration", the latter ignored scientific progress accomplished since Engels' death and showed no interest in "bourgeois science", except for the sake of polemics. What deserved a thorough inquiry, Ossowski commented, was the astonishing ossification of the Marxist-Leninist philosophical and sociological doctrine, which strangely contrasted with its progressive political and social program. Ossowski set out to accomplish this task in two impressive essays [7].

Ossowski's critical examination of Marxism-Leninism was one of many attempts undertaken by non-Marxist scholars to discuss the foundations of the Marxist-Lenist doctrines (Ajdukiewicz, Chałasiński, Kłósak, Kotarbiński, Łubnicki). Although only Ossowski received an answer, the efforts of the others were not wasted. In particular, Ajdukiewicz's skilful performance played a considerable part in modifying the Marxist-Leninist doctrine at a later period [8].

Łubnicki's two essays were the most comprehensive examination of Marxist-Leninist philosophy as a whole [9]. His criticism can ultimately be reduced to laying bare the incompatibility of Marxian positivism and naturalism with what it retained from Hegel's philosophy.

It was generally pointed out that these Hegelian survivals have been taken over and put into relief by Marxism-Leninism, which revives metaphysical disputes of the last century and presents their solutions, now only of historical value, as a final and scientifically valid theory of the universe, society, history and man's place in nature. Marxism-Leninism abounds in vague and equivocal concepts, ambiguous and untestable assumptions, fallacious arguments, ideas derived from antiquated science, logic and methodology. If the meaning of Engels' various statements were examined, their implications analysed and concepts made unequivocal, many misconceptions would have disappeared. Since this has not been done, the valuable trends in the Marxian tradition – its rejection, in principle, of speculative philosophy, its insistence that only experience and reason provide valid knowledge, and that philosophy can contribute to an effective action, transforming social and historical reality – are submerged by naive and uncritical conceptions, accepted on the strength of practical considerations or emotions rather than of logical arguments.

The second period is known under the name of the "times of the cult of personality" or the "Stalinist period". Its commencement was not initiated by any new development in the realm of thought. It was closely bound up, to use the words of A. Schaff, the leading Marxist-Leninist philosopher in Poland, with the "progress of the class struggle and of the socialist construction in our country". The event that ushered in the new era in philosophy was the setting up of the Polish Workers' United Party at the end of 1948. Following it, Marxism-Leninism was announced to be the Party's and State's official doctrine, enforced by all the administrative means at the disposal of the authorities. Marxism-Leninism could no longer be freely discussed and criticised in public, the validity of its foundations and the main body of its doctrine were placed beyond suspicion and possible human doubt (unless the revision or re-adjustment was made by the highest Marxist-Leninist authority in or outside the country). The Stalinist period in philosophy and science commenced in 1949 and was officially inaugurated at the First Congress of Polish Science, held in Warsaw early in 1951.

In the period under discussion Marxist-Leninists were no longer a handful of politicians, journalists and ideologists, active outside of the universities and the world of learning. Many of them were appointed to university chairs. Their ranks increased by the adherence of some non-Marxist scholars and, above all, by a large and growing number of younger people, some of them of outstanding ability (B. Baczko, H. Eilstein, L. Kołakowski).

The Stalinist period was not, as it might be thought, a period of complete stagnation. Much was happening beneath the surface which, in the course of time, has shaken the very foundations of Marxism-Leninism in Poland. The Stalinist period was unfruitful in the sense that it did not produce anything philosophically significant and impeded any development of philosophical thought. The battle of quotations and the repetition of threadbare clichés supplanted logical analysis and rational argument. These were the years of solemn boredom, and also of establishing philosophical truths by oracular pronouncements and governmental decrees. A codified, doctrinaire rationalism had no use for intellectual curiosity, knowledge and inventive skill. The Stalinist period ended as it had begun, namely by political events of a revolutionary character.

These events took place, however, after Marxism-Leninism had already been changed out of recognition from within, and abandoned by its most promising exponents, who have returned to Marx and the Marxian tradition. Marxism-Leninism disintegrated in Poland and left very few clinging to the flotsam and jetsam of the intellectual shipwreck. The first signs of what was forthcoming appeared in 1954, and the following year the disintegration was practically complete. The whole structure was so badly damaged by the moving ground of critical thought beneath it that it could not stand the slightest strain and collapsed at the first stress.

This was the beginning of the third period, now in progress, which in some respects is reminiscent of the first. It cannot be described in general terms, since it has not yet acquired any characteristic features, apart from the fact that in contradistinction to the past Marxism-Leninism is only one among a number of philosophical points of view or schools of thought.

During the Stalinist period Marxist-Leninist philosophers were writing profusely. They themselves now recognise that these were the "times of errors and deviations" and do not attach much importance to what they published. There is no reason to disagree with this assessment.

With one single exception, Polish Marxist-Leninists did not make any original contribution to the Marxist-Leninist doctrine. The exception is Schaff's "Some Problems of the Marxist Theory of Truth" [10]. No larger work dealing with the concept of truth from the Marxist-Leninist point of view ever appeared either in the Soviet Union or elsewhere, and Schaff's study, its title notwithstanding, is the first exhaustive monograph on the subject. Although it is clearly a contribution to Marxist-Leninist philosophy alone, it makes considerable use of views worked out in Poland by Twardowski, Kotarbiński, Ajdukiewicz and Tarski.

The Polish version of Marxist-Leninist philosophy had, however, a number of peculiar characteristics. At first, they took the form of certain minor deviations or shifts of emphasis. Since instead of disappearing they persisted and tended to increase the original distance from orthodoxy, in the course of time they have produced a markedly different Marxist-Leninist philosophy from that existing in the Soviet Union.

The first and most important was the problem of the relation of dialectics to formal logic. The fundamental premiss of Marxist-Leninist philosophy is the assumption that internal contradictions are inherent in all things and phenomena of nature. This implies that the principle of non-contradiction and formal logic in general should be either altogether rejected or severely restricted, to be replaced by dialectics, an entirely new method of thinking, peculiar, as Engels believed, to a higher stage of the mind's development. In this manner, Marxist-Leninist philosophy has exposed itself to an easy criticism and to the objection of absurdity. A logically trained philosopher has no use for a system that denies the principle of non-contradiction. Let us assume that two statements like "p" and "~ p" are true together. Then, by means of a well-known formula of the propositional calculus: p. ⊃ . ~ p ⊃ q, we can by applying the detachment rule twice derive from these contradictory premises an arbitrary statement "q", i.e. any statement whatsoever. Thus, true and false statements turn out to be equally valid and the difference between truth and falsehood vanishes.

The burden of this truth-destroying doctrine, defended for a few years, proved to be too heavy for Marxist-Leninists in Poland. Faced by logically trained philosophers, they were at once driven on the defensive. They could spread and popularise their views among the philosophically uninstructed and naive, but those with scientific training could not be really persuaded to accept Marxist-Leninist philosophy as a sound and justifiable system of beliefs. A Marxist-Leninist was tainted with absurdity through the mere enunciation of his fundamental principles. This was increasingly recognised by Marxist-Leninists in Poland and, finally (1955), the orthodox views on the principle of non-contradiction and formal logic were repudiated by practically all Polish Marxist-Leninists. As Schaff explained, Marx, Engels, Lenin and their followers were misled by Hegel and mistook contraries for contradictories. A sharp distinction should be made between a logical and a dialectical contradiction, for the latter is not a contradiction *sensu stricto*.[11]

The second difference between the Soviet and Polish versions of Marxist-Leninist philosophy had to do with the principle of *partijnost'* (partisanship). This principle assumes the social determination of all knowledge and its variable validity depending on the social location of particular socio-economic classes. In the course of social and historical development different classes occupy a social location that is situationally adequate for knowledge to be valid (or as valid as it is possible under the existing historical and social circumstances). It is claimed that, at present, only the proletariat provides a social location that favours progress of genuine and undistorted knowledge. This knowledge has been attained by the proletarian party, that is, by the Communist Party, which is by definition the most conscious and advanced part of the proletariat. *"Partijnost'"* is usually defined as "to be in agreement with the objective truth", provided it is understood that "objective truth" is what is declared by the Party leadership to be true in each particular case. A non-Party scholar and scientist may also rise to the "objective truth", when he is in accord with the Party, accepts its authority to determine what is and what is not knowledge and to settle scientific questions recognised by the Party to be its concern.

From the very beginning, Polish Marxist-Leninists suffered from the handicap of being aware that the principle of *partijnost'* is unsound and cannot be maintained by any consistent and valid argument. It was an unenviable task, complained some young university lecturers in Marxism-Leninism, to face the undergraduates with the statement that the Marxist-Leninist doctrine is objectively true and partisan at the same time [12]. It was not difficult to show that whatever political significance is attached to the principle of *partijnost'*, it is factually false and formally untenable [13]. For it clearly involves what is commonly called the "genetic fallacy" and the "relativist fallacy".

In 1956 the principle of *partijnost'* was repudiated by the young former supporters of the orthodox doctrine (H. Eilstein, L. Kołakowski). It was also re-examined in terms of the sociology of science and the methodology of the social sciences by Ossowski and his pupil, A. Malewski [14]. As a result of these combined efforts it is unlikely that it will ever recover.

The "dual theory of ideology" (which can be briefly described as the doctrine that there is the bourgeois and necessarily fraudulent and reactionary science, and the proletarian and necessarily objectively true and progressive science), closely associated with the principle of *partijnost'*, still nominally survives in Polish Marxism-Leninism but has been changed out of recognition. For it claims no more than that in the social sciences there are two qualitatively different ideological attitudes – the progressive and the conservative. Between these two extremes there are intermediate attitudes, in various respects closer either to one or the other of the extremes. The two basic attitudes are conceived as ideal types in Max Weber's sense rather than as actual attitudes ever to be found in a pure form in experience. There is no longer the question of confusing the social and psychological origin of a belief with its logical validity [15].

The third peculiarity of the Polish version of Marxist-Leninist philosophy

94

was its anti-Hegelian orientation. It is true that under Stalin the anti-Hegelian trend in the Soviet Marxism-Leninism was conspicuous, and its reflection in the Polish version was to be expected. But there is little doubt that the influence was at least strongly reinforced by native considerations. The intellectual climate of Polish philosophy was decidedly hostile to the speculations of Hegelian metaphysics. Hegel's doctrine was thought to be pernicious, his method fantastic and capable of producing any farrago of nonsense. Schaff, the leading Marxist-Leninist philosopher in Poland and the chief exponent of the anti-Hegelian orientation, was sensitive to the impact of these opinions. Although it might be doubted whether Marxism-Leninism can ever be emancipated from the Hegelian heritage, the expurgation from it of the most objectionable Hegelian influences did mark a certain progress of Marxism-Leninism towards common-sense and reason.

The anti-Hegelian tendency was not a universal phenomenon. Some Marxist-Leninists or former Marxist-Leninists of the younger generation, mainly those interested in the history of social and philosophical thought, were admirers of Hegel (Baczko, Kołakowski, Kroński). The Hegelian wing was motivated not only by respect for Hegel's historical dialectics but also by the desire to find an escape from the intellectual straight-jacket imposed on Marxist-Leninist historians by Ždanov's methodological rules of historical inquiry [16]. There is little doubt that it was Hegel who helped them to realise the crudity and intellectual arrogance of Ždanov's pronouncements. At present, historians of philosophy of the Marxist-Leninist intellectual formation have remained under Hegel's influence and something like a Hegelian revival is apparent among them.

Today, it is hardly possible to say that there is a Marxist-Leninist doctrine in Poland. There are Marxist-Leninists who differ from each other less than from the scientifically and logically minded philosophers, the founders and descendants of the tradition established by the Warsaw school in the inter-war period. But, among themselves, Polish Marxist-Leninists differ considerably and they do not subscribe to the same body of views. There are different orientations among them which criss-cross each other. For, apart from the Hegelian and anti-Hegelian tendencies, there is also the traditionalist and revisionist, the positivist and anti-positivist wing. "Positivism" is used here in its 19th century meaning and refers to its somewhat restricted form, in which it can be found in some of the writings of Marx and Engels in contradistinction to those of Lenin and Stalin.

Marxist-Leninist philosophers in Poland continue to differ essentially from the scientifically minded philosophers both by their method of thinking and the range of their interests. Their method has remained traditionalistic, unaffected by the development of modern logic, methodology and philosophy of language. Their main concern continues to be problems of the view of the world or ideology, that is, beliefs that offer a synoptic understanding of the universe, society and man's place in his natural and human environment.

This particular approach to, or conception of, philosophy has produced one outstanding and original thinker. Leszek Kołakowski, now in his early thirties, was once a militant supporter of the Marxist-Leninist doctrine but has now become one of its most determined and incisive critics. His knowledge, within a certain range of interests, is wide and accurate, his mind knows no dogmas and follows the argument wherever it might lead him. He can perhaps best be described as a philosopher of life, rooted in the Marxian tradition. For Marx's "vibrant philosophical inspiration", as he himself stated, affects his whole way of looking at the world [17]. He is anxious to explore problems which his scientifically minded contemporaries – Z. Czezwinski, J. Giedymin, T. Pawłowski, J. Pelc, M. Przełęcki, K. Szaniawski – prefer to avoid because of their being inaccessible to a precise formulation and incapable of elucidation by exact methods.

The present philosophical scene in Poland is varied and lively. There is a thriving and numerous school of mathematical logic which, under the undisputed leadership of Mostowski, enjoys an international reputation. A two-volume collection of important and previously not easily accessible essays of Kotarbiński was published and followed by his new work "Lectures on the History of Logic", one of the most comprehensive contributions to the history of logic from the modern viewpoint available in world literature [18]. Ajdukiewicz continues to write his enlightening, painstaking analyses of specific issues in the field of logic, methodology and philosophy of language. Czeżowski resumed the publication of *"Ruch Filozoficzny"*, closed down by administrative order in 1950, and republished some of his works and articles [19]. There appeared two volumes of Ingarden's essays and the first Polish edition of his *"Das literarische Kunstwerk"* [20]. Tatarkiewicz's "History of Philosophy", withdrawn from circulation in the Stalinist past, had another edition [21]. Ossowska published a learned monograph on "Bourgeois Morality" and Ossowski emerged from an obscurity imposed by administrative measures with a remarkable work, "Class Structure in Social Consciousness" [22]. Works of A. Krokiewicz, a distinguished historian of ancient philosophy, of J. Lande, L. Petrażycki and Cz. Znamierowski, theorists of law and moral philosophers, which were either banned or did not receive the *nihil obstat* of the Communist authorities, appeared or re-appeared in the years 1956–1959 [23]. Christian philosophers were able to increase and develop their activities. Since the end of the war, some of them have contributed to the development of logic, history of logic and history of philosophy (J. Iwanicki, J. Kalinowski, S. Kamiński, K. Kłósak, S. Mazierski, S. Świeżawski), and all have earned recognition, in the outside world too, for the collective achievements of the school and the enrichment of Christian thought. In particular, M. A. Krąpiec enjoys the reputation of a highly original mind and his two works, published since 1956, are considered as notable contributions to Christian philosophy [24]. Philosophers of various schools of thought contribute to *"Studia Filozoficzne"*, the chief philosophical publication in the country. *"Studia Logica"*, a yearly logical publication, of which eight volumes have appeared, is widely known to logicians all over the world.

These are hopeful signs and the upsurge of energy is remarkable, but it is too early to see the shape of things to come.

REFERENCES

1. This is a partial summary of a larger study, "Philosophy and Ideology" (to appear soon in the series "Sovietica"), which, in addition to describing the philosophical developments in Poland in the years 1918–1958, includes a critical examination of the logical, methodological and epistemological theories of Marxist-Leninist philosophy.
2. See, e.g., Nagel, E.: *Logic without Metaphysics*. Glencoe (Ill.). 1956. pp. 192–197 and 241–246. Joergensen, J.: *The Development of Logical Positivism*. IEUS vol. 2, No. 9. Chicago. 1951. pp. 54–55. Beth, E. W.: *Les fondements logiques des mathématiques* (Collection de Logique Mathématique). Paris. 1955.
3. Killed by the Germans.
4. The most comprehensive account of the philosophical development in Poland in the inter-war period is to be found in Bocheński, J. M: *La philosophie*. In: *Pologne 1919–1939*, vol. 3: *Vie intellectuelle et artistique*. Neuchatel. 1947. pp. 229–260. A more specialized survey is provided by Ajdukiewicz, K.: *Der logistische Antiirrationalismus in Polen*. In: Erkenntnis 5, 1935, 151–161. Jordan, Z.: *The Development of Mathematical Logic and of Logical Positivism in Poland between the Two Wars*. London. 1945, covers very much the same ground as Ajdukiewicz's survey but in greater detail.
5. See, e.g., Gromska, D.: *Philosophes polonais morts entre 1938 et 1945*. Studia Philosophica 3, 1939–1946, 31–97. For a more comprehensive, but not exhaustive, list of those who died in the period September 1939 – March 1946, see Olszewicz, B.: *Lista strat kultury polskiej*. Warszawa. Wydawnictwo S. Arcta. 1947. The list includes scholars, scientists, artists, men of letters, politicians, doctors, technicians and other members of the professional classes. The list comprises some 4,400 names. About half of those listed were either shot by the firing-squads of the German army or perished in the concentration camps. All the universities were closed down, many libraries were destroyed or removed to Germany. The same applies to the equipment of research institutes. Individuals suffered losses to their private book collections and manuscripts of works prepared for publication. In the Warsaw rising (1944) a whole generation of graduates and young research-workers, some of them of great promise, was decimated in the fighting against the Germans or exterminated by atrocities inflicted upon the population of the devastated but unconquered city.
6. Mostowski, A.: *Logika Matematyczna (Polskie Towarzystwo Matematyczne, Monografie Matematyczne* T. 18*)*. Warszawa-Wrocław. 1948. Czeżowski, T.: *Logika. Podręcznik dla studiujących nauki filozoficzne*. Warszawa. 1949. Ossowska, M.: *Podstawy nauki o moralności*. Warszawa. 1947. and *Motywy postępowania. Z zagadnień psychologii moralności*. Warszawa. 1949. Tatarkiewicz, Wł.: *Historia filozofii*. T. 3. *Filozofia XIX wieku i współczesna*. Krakow. 1950. Ingarden, R.: *Spór o istnienie świata*. T. 1. Krakow. 1947. T. 2. 1948.
7. Ossowski, St.: *Doktryna marksistowska na tle dzisiejszej epoki*. Myśl Współczesna 1947, 12/19, 501–513; *Teoretyczne zadanie marksizmu. Szkic programu*. Myśl Współczesna 1948, 1/20, 3–18.
8. Ajdukiewicz, K.: *Zmiana i sprzeczność*. Myśl Współczesna 1948, 8–9/27–28, 35–52.
9. Łubnicki, N.: *Teoria poznania materializmu dialektycznego*. Annales Universitatis Mariae Curie-Skłodowska, Sectio F, Vol. 1, 1946 (2), 121–186; *Epistemological Problems of Dialectical Materialism*. Synthèse 7, 1948–1949 (4–5), 274–296.
10. Schaff, A.: *Z zagadnień marksistowskiej teorii prawdy*. Warszawa. 1951.

11. Schaff, A.: *Dialektyka marksistowska a zasada sprzeczności*. Myśl Filozoficzna 1955, 4/18, 143–158.
12. Eilstein, H., Kochański, Z.: *O projekcie programu materializmu dialektycznego*. Myśl Filozoficzna 1956, 3/23, 151.
13. Chałasiński, J.: *Socjologia polska w latach międzywojennych a prądy społeczne i umysłowe*. Myśl Współczesna 1949, 1–2/32–33, 11–13. Lange, O.: *The Scope and Method of Economics*. In: Feigl, H., Brodbeck, M. (eds.): *Readings in the Philosophy of Science*. N. Y. 1953. 750–751. Ossowski, St.: *Marksizm i tworczość naukowa w społeczeństwie socjalistycznym* Artykuły z lat 1947–1956 (Biblioteczka Po Prostu 11). Warszawa. 1957, 71–74.
14. Ossowski, St.: *Marksizm i tworczość naukowa w społeczeństwie socjalistycznym*. Artykuły z lat 1947–1956, 78–99. Malewski, A.: *Postulaty praktycznej uzyteczności a rozwój nauk społecznych*. (Zeszyty Naukowe Uniwersytetu A. Mickiewicza Nr. 5, Filozofia Z. 1). Poznań. 1956, 3–13.
15. Lange, O.: *Ekonomia polityczna*. T. 1. *Zagadnienia ogolne*. Warszawa. 1959, 276–292.
16. See, e.g., Baczko, B., Kołakowski, L.: *Tradycje naukowe socjalizmu i zadania marksistowskiej historiografii filozoficznej*. Myśl Filozoficzna 1954, 4/14, 78–103.
17. Kołakowski, L.: *Permanent and Transitory Aspects of Marxism*. In: Mayewski, P. (ed.): *The Broken Mirror. A Collection of Writings from Contemporary Poland*. N. Y. 1958.
18. Kotarbiński, T.: *Wybór pism*. T. 1. Warszawa. 1957. T. 2. 1958; *Wykłady z dziejow logiki* (Łódzkie Towarzystwo Naukowe, Wydz. 1, Nr. 28). Łódz. 1957.
19. Czeżowski, T.: *Odczyty filozoficzne (Towarzystwo Naukowe w Toruniu, Prace Wydziału Filologiczno-Filozoficznego, T. 7)*. Toruń. 1958; *Głowne zasady nauk filozoficznych, Wydanie trzecie poprawione i rozszerzone*. Wrocław. 1959. "*Ruch Filozoficzny*" is a bibliographical periodical, which gives information on the philosophical developments at home and abroad. It was started by K. Twardowski in 1911.
20. Ingarden, R.: *Studie z estetyki*. T. 1. Warszawa. 1957. T. 2. 1958; *O dziele literackim. Badania z pogranicza ontologii, teorii języka i filozofii literatury*. Warszawa. 1960. Ingarden, Tatarkiewicz, Ossowska and Ossowski were sent on enforced leave of absence and they could neither teach nor publish anything during the Stalinist period.
21. Tatarkiewicz, Wł.: *Historia filozofii*. T. 1–3. Warszawa. 1959.
22. Ossowska, M.: *Moralność mieszczańska* (Łódzkie Towarzystwo Naukowe, Wydz. 1, Nr. 22). Łodz. 1956. Ossowski, St.: *Struktura klasowa w społecznej świadomości* (Łódzkie Towarzystwo Naukowe, Wydz. 2, Nr. 21). Łódz. 1957.
23. Krokiewicz, A.: *Sokrates*. Warszawa. 1958. Lande, J.: *Studia z filozofii prawa*. Warszawa. 1959. Petrażycki, L.: *Wstęp do nauki prawa i moralności*. Warszawa. 1959; *Teoria prawa i państwa*. T. 1. Warszawa. 1959. Znamierowski, Cz.: *Oceny i normy*. Warszawa. 1957; *Zasady i kierunki etyki*. Warszawa. 1957.
24 Krąpiec, M. A.: *Realizm ludzkiego poznania*. Poznań. 1959; *Teoria analogii bytu (Towarzystwo Naukowe KUL, Rozprawy Wydziału Filozoficznego 9)*. Lublin. 1959. Pastuszka, J.: *Charakter człowieka. Struktura, typologia, diagnostyka psychologiczna*. Lublin. 1959 should be mentioned as the third major work published by Christian thinkers since 1956.

MARXISM-LENINISM IN CZECHOSLOVAKIA *

(1) METHODOLOGICAL. The subject of this paper is philosophy in Com-
munist-controlled Czechoslovakia. Here philosophy is taken in the academic sense of the word; hence, purely dogmatic or tactically conditioned
materials – e.g. as found in Party resolutions, addresses by certain politically inclined university professors, etc. – are not taken into consideration.[1]
Aside from this, the author is of the opinion that, at least since 1950, every
philosophically relevant publication can be classed under the heading
"Marxist-Leninist Philosophy in the ČSR". For the domain of professional philosophy is, in Czechoslovakia as in the USSR, so unequivocally Com-
munist-controlled that even purely formal publications [2] which seemingly
fall outside the scope of Marxism-Leninism must, in reality, be valued as
indices of this very Marxism-Leninism in Czechoslovakia. That such a
supposition is in no way self-evident can be seen from the situation in
Poland. Since R. Ingarden, a disciple of Husserl, and the logician K. Ajdukiewicz[3] are teaching at the University of Cracow and lectures on Marxism-
Leninism are unknown, and since not long ago M. A. Krąpiec,[4] a Thomist
and Dominican, was able to publish an excellent work, there seems to be
little sense in trying to force all the philosophic phenomena of contemporary Poland under the heading "Marxism-Leninism".

(2) SOURCES. At present two technical journals of philosophy are published
in Czechoslovakia. "Filosofický časopis", published by the Institute of Philosophy of the Czechoslovak Academy of Sciences (ČSAV), first appeared
in April 1953 as a quarterly. Since the beginning of 1956 it has appeared
six times a year and by the end of 1959 approximately 4,800 pages had
appeared. "Slovenský filozofický časopis", published by the Slovak Academy of Sciences (SAV) (Institute of Philosophy), first appeared in 1946
under the title "Philosophia Slovaca" and, although Communist from the
outset, it came under strict Communist control in 1949. It is a quarterly at

* Lobkowicz, N.: Marxismus-Leninismus in der ČSR (Sovietica, Abhandlungen).
Dordrecht (in preparation). The present article was first published in Zeitschrift für
Ostforschung (Kiel) 1960, 2/3.

present and by the end of 1959 some 4,200 pages had been published. In addition, *"Sovětská věda – Filosofie"*, published by the philosophic section of the Czechoslovak-Soviet Institute (Prague), appeared six times a year from 1951 to 1955 and the total production was about 3,200 pages.[5] Discounting the numerous translations and works of a popular nature, there were some 50 technical philosophical publications in book form, among which a number were of several hundred pages. Finally, there were numerous articles of a philosophical or ideological character in *"Rudé Právo"*,[6] in the Party organ *"Nová Mysl"*, in cultural periodicals such as *"Tvorba"*, *"Literární Noviny"*[7], etc., as well as philosophically relevant articles in historical and legal periodicals and articles on questions of logistic and the philosophical interpretation of mathematics [8] in journals of mathematics and the natural sciences.

(3) PERIODS. The history of Marxist-Leninist philosophy in Czechoslovakia falls, as I see it, into three main periods: 1. From the foundation of the Czech and Slovak Communist Party (1920/21) to the end of the Second World War; 2. From 1945 (for Slovakia already the end of 1944) to the establishment of the two academies of sciences (1952/53); 3. From 1953 to the present. Seen from the point of view of the history of philosophy, the year 1948 – which was politically very significant – is not of too much importance since, on the one hand, there were important centres for the teaching of Marxist-Leninist philosophy already before 1948 and, on the other, it was quite a while after 1948 before the Marxist-Leninists were in definite control of the ideological domain. A Communist commentator correctly characterized the situation when, in 1956, he wrote: "Marxist philosophy began to receive special attention as a theoretical discipline and object of higher education for the first time after the revolution of 1945 ... Scientific Marxist philosophy began to be consciously developed for the first time after February 1948, but only the establishment of philosophical institutes in 1953 permitted a transition to calm and systematic specialized work." [9]

(4) HISTORICAL SKETCH. As far as the first period is concerned, one can hardly speak of an independent Marxist-Leninist philosophy – this is explicitly conceded today. The most interesting part of it is the time to 1931 (the condemnation of A. M. Joffes, known under the pseudonym Deborin!). J. Kabeš, later Minister of Finance, published in 1925 an intelligent article on Masaryk and socialism [10], and in 1926 a discussion on

the essence of fascism appeared on the pages of *"Kommunistická Revue"*. Among the Czechs, in addition to the above-mentioned J. Kabeš (whose pseudonym, J. Tábor, is taken from his birth-place), must be mentioned P. Reiman and L. Svoboda [11] and among the Slovaks we find E. Urx, who was put to death at Mauthausen in 1942, and L. Szántó. These names suffice to show that before the war it was more a question of philosophic journalism [12] than of pure philosophy. In any case, we must admit that our information on this period is very fragmentary – the sources mentioned above, especially the *"Komunistická Revue"*, are not now available in the West.

The lack of specialists was also determining in the first years after 1945. The older Communists had more important things to do than philosophy and, further, they had no academic qualifications. As far as the philosophers who went over to Communism are concerned, the fact is that they understood very little of orthodox Marxism-Leninism. Strictly speaking, there was, in the first years after the war, only one single man in all of Czechoslovakia who could be termed, without any reserves, a professional philosopher and an orthodox Marxist-Leninist. He was A. Kolman, a Russian of Czech origin, who had become acquainted with Nejedlý in the Soviet Union and who was appointed professor at the Karls-University in 1945. In addition to Kolman there was L. Štoll, who was teaching at the newly-founded college for political and social sciences (Prague). A journalist, he was later to become Minister of Education. In 1948 when Kolman returned to the Soviet Union (rumour has it, because of friction with the CPČ [13]) L. Svoboda took his university post. In Slovakia there was no Kolman to be found. Although Communist penetration of the University of Pressburg was faster than that in Prague, the leading Marxist-Leninist philosophers were (and are till today), without exception, personalities who were unknown as Communists before 1943. Yet the Philosophical Institute of the old SAVU [14], founded in January 1946 by I. Hrušovský, was strongly infected by Communism.

In 1950 the last non-Communist professors, among them the most important professor of philosophy of the first republic, J. Král, were eliminated. By 1953, the era of the founding of both academies of science, there was already a small group of young Communist professional philosophers. Thenceforward the development is continuous and unmarked by significant events – such things as "thaws" are hardly to be found. Significant, though, is the fact that as of 1956 the level rose considerably and the dogmatic atmosphere cleared slightly. At the beginning of 1959 there was a sort of clean-up operation in which L. Tondl, up to then uncontested intellectual chief of the philosophers at the Karls-University, and some others (e.g. I. Sviták) who had remained anonymous up to that time, were accused of the previously unknown deviation of "positivistic revisionism", and removed.[15] The deeper reasons for this change, in which an entire series of unknown names appeared, are still not clear today.

(5) THE PERSONALITIES. First a distinction must be made between philosophizing party men and professional philosophers. In the first group belong, almost without exception, all the philosophizing old Communists like L. Štoll, L. Svoboda and L. Szántó, but also most of those philosophers who held important positions, such as A. Sirácky (president of the SAV) or M. Topol'ský (at that time rector of the Comenius-University). In the first years after the war these men were *the* Marxist-Leninist philosophers; from about 1955 on, although they contributed a discourse or editorial here and there, not much was heard from them and they are not mentioned as philosophers. The professional philosophers are divided into several groups. Communist publications divide them, for the most part, according to age, [16] but a grouping according to field of interest (e.g. Marxist-Leninist philosophy in general, logic, aesthetics, history of philosophy, etc.) is also possible. The distribution according to age is sensible because the older professional philosophers are, almost without exception, latter-day Communists – for example, the former neo-Kantian L. Rieger (1890–1958), associate professor before the war and, from 1953 to shortly before his death, director of the Philosophic Institute of the ČSAV; I. Hrušovský (b. 1908), former neo-Positivist (of the Vienna circle), from 1946 on director of the Philosophic Institute of the SAV and the most politically experienced of the professional philosophers; J. Popelová-Otáhalová (b. 1904), disciple of Vl. Hoppe (1882–1931) (the religiously oriented Brünn-positivist), post-war rector of the Palacký-University in Olomouc, today occupying the chair of history of philosophy at the Karls-University; M. Novák (b. 1901), who began teaching aesthetics in the thirties and is today professor in Prague; O. Zich (b. 1908), who habilitated in 1948 with a significant work on logic and who occupies the recently (1 August 1958) established chair for logic in Prague. With the possible exception of J. Popelová, not one of them was a Communist before 1945, let alone a member of the Party. They learned their Communism after the war [17], came into the limelight about

1953 and quickly became prominent. The middle generation (born somewhere between 1915 and 1930) is ideologically so strongly committed that very often there is no distinction between party ideologist and professional philosopher. Here we find, for example, the majority of the historians of Czech philosophy – like, M. Machovec, follower of Nejedlý, and R. Kalivoda [18], the expert on Hus; further, teachers like J. Cvekl, K. Kosík, L. Hanzel, Dr. Slejška and V. Ruml, who was chief editor of the "Filosofický časopis" as of 1955 [19]. The grouping according to specialities is clearest among the younger generation. We find specialists for the history of ancient logic, for logistic, for certain problems of aesthetics, for short periods of the history of philosophy, etc. Once in a while, we find non-Communists who have managed to keep their posts – for example, J. B. Kozák, a positivist from a protestant theological background, or K. Svoboda, [20] who is a philologist and important historian of aesthetics. Such non-Communists, among whom must be also counted E. Utitz (d. 3 November 1956), who was a student of Husserl and a German-speaking aesthetician, are able to print little – once in a while a neutral book, a small article, or a book review. Most of the time, they work as translators (in addition to Kozák and K. Svoboda we find the Aristotle expert, A. Kříž). Since 1957 even those professors who had lost their positions were treated with more consideration, as can be seen from the cases of the sociologist, A. Štefánek, and of J. Král in 1959.

(6) THEMES. Since about 1956 the most intensive work has been done on questions which are only incidental to ideology: logic, aesthetics, history of philosophy. In Diahistomat, interest has centred on the essence of the popular democracies [21] and significant work has been done in this respect. In the last few years logic has taken on great importance, which is evidenced by the fact that the leading Czech logicians are members of the big organizations such as the editorial staffs of the technical journals. Already in 1948 Kolman had published an interesting work on logistic [22]. Today the leader is O. Zich, who in 1956 published a widely-discussed investigation of the logical structure of popular sayings [23]. Other important logicians are: K. Berka, P. Materna, M. Mleziva, O. Weinberger and, above all, the young Slovak, V. Filkorn [24]. Peripheral areas of logic such as the philosophy of mathematics and cybernetics (for which a special commission was set up in 1958) are also treated. In aesthetics the questions are mainly of a formal character and discussions usually take the form of arguments with

E. Hostinský, the leading pre-war Czech aesthetician. The most original work in the history of philosophy is done in ancient and contemporary philosophy. Little work is done on the Renaissance, the Enlightenment or the 19th century – here, there is a great dependence on the Soviet version. In ancient philosophy, the translations are of great interest: Aristotle's "Categories" and "Peri Hermeneias", Galen's introduction to logic, the "Lives and Opinions" of Diogenes Laertius, etc. In addition, there are many valuable articles which could have as well appeared in Western journals.[25] The most significant achievement in Czech history of philosophy was the publication of the Arabic text and commented French translation of the previously unpublished "Psychology" of Avicenna [26]. Up to the present, the Soviets have produced no such technical advancements. And the Czech contributions on contemporary Anglo-Saxon philosophy (pragmatism, neo-positivism) seem to surpass what is being done in the Soviet Union. In any case, two such books are among the rare technically philosophical Czech works which have been translated into Russian [27].

A distinct and very difficult chapter is the history of Czech philosophy. As Minister of Education, Nejedlý in a speech on 29 January 1946 chided the professional philosophers for their decadence and required that they turn their attention to philosophizing scientists, poets and even composers (Smetana!). This thesis first took effect in 1950 [28]. After that, one studied the "philosophic outlooks" of people like the poets Kollár and Štúr, the enlightener Dobrovský, the scientists Purkyně and Procházka, and, of course, Nejedlý himself. Nejedlý's prestige began to decline with the rejection of the cult of personality in 1956 (which was rare among Czech philosophers even in reference to President Gottwald, but common in reference to Nejedlý) and attention turned to real philosophers such as B. Bolzano (who is considered Czech), A. Smetana (an excommunicated Knight of the Cross who developed a highly fantastic metaphysics à la Schelling and, in social theory, stood close to the Hegelian left), J. Krejčí, and more recently, philosophers of the first republic. In the Bohemian lands, the ideological battle took the form of opposition to "Masarykism"; since 1954, the theory of Nejedlý and Kopecký, according to which the young Masaryk was "relatively progressive" [29], is violently opposed. In Slovakia the opposition was to "Hlasism", which is interpreted as the "Slovak variation of Masarykism", and especially to the so-called "ľudactví" who are made to include not only the "clerico-fascism" of Hlinka's Populist

Party of the so-called Slovak State (1939–1944) but also educated Catholics in general [30].
(7) ORGANIZATION AND SPIRIT. Here it would be of interest to describe the organisation and atmosphere in which philosophy is developed in Czechoslovakia.
(a) Since, as of 1953, the "Czechoslovak Society for the Spread of Political and Scientific Knowledge" took care of teaching, vulgarisation and popularisation of Marxism-Leninism, the ČSAV and the SAV [31] were able to devote themselves completely to scientific research and publication. At the same time, these institutes granted academic degrees, thus providing new blood. Here the youngest generation of philosophers comes into its own – while they are working on their theses as candidates or doctors, they are accepted as colleagues of the Institute and financially supported. Each year the Slovak Institute publishes a report of the meetings held, works published and projects under way. The Czech Institute publishes no such bulletin but does issue a list of the works undertaken (including those written in the higher schools).
(b) Great stress is laid on team-work, at least in the Institutes.[32] Many articles and books carry the names of two or even more authors and every work is thoroughly criticised before publication. This explains the polite and even friendly tone of discussion, especially since 1956. Outside of this, many of the discussions are quite sharp (but not personal [33]) – on many questions there is no unity and the discussion can last for as long as a year. The most interesting of these discussions was solved by the young philosopher J. Bartoš, who, in Spring 1957, took the lead of the Pole, A. Schaff, in criticising Engels' version of local motion and, through this, Lenin's doctrine of the "unity of continuity and discontinuity", as "simple phrases"[34]. There were further discussions on the nature of popular democracy, on the interpretation of Czech history of philosophy, etc.
(c) A comparison of Czech Marxism-Leninism with the Soviet form is, at least partially, in favour of the Czech works. The conversion of many of the older professors to Communism has, no doubt, much to do with this. Yet one can hardly speak of a higher level of Marxism-Leninism itself. It is more a question of the superiority of Czech specialists of history of philosophy – an advantage which is evident only in the peripheral disciplines but which prevents any massive judgements such as are the *"mot d'ordre"* in the Soviet Union. In addition, we find in Czechoslovakia a

basic readiness to objectively examine Western technical works.[35] A further important point is the almost universal recognition of formal logic and its laws. Here we see the effect of the positivist tradition in the older Czech philosophy. This does not mean that the dialectic or dialectical logic is simply rejected – rather, the dialectic is interpreted in a formal-logical or even logistic manner [36]. In general, the Czech logicians have it easier than their Soviet counterparts since they are part of the elite and not suspected outsiders. A knowledge of the history of philosophy, a readiness to examine Western works, and the recognition of formal logic are the principal reasons why Czech Marxism-Leninism cannot afford to simply reject the Western origins of its Bohemian and Slovak cultures – a circumstance which is to the advantage of the general level of contemporary Czech philosophy. At the same time, Czech philosophers tend to be critical, not without justification, of the Czech philosophic tradition, which is, especially as regards Czech pre-war philosophy, condemned for its eclecticism [37], its woolliness [38], and its "aestheticizing" attitude.

(8) CONCLUSION. While it had seemed that the Communists had not succeeded in establishing a living Marxist-Leninist philosophy in Czechoslovakia, today one must recognize their important success. The philosophic team [39] is, it is true, not large, but its representatives seem to be uncompromisingly Communist, on the one hand, and seriously philosophical, on the other. That there is seldom a conflict is comprehensible when one takes into account the fact that the themes treated have little to do with ideological matters and are, for the most part, treated with professional seriousness.

REFERENCES

1. In a world where technical philosophy always has political overtones and politics ideological colouring, such a limitation is not always easy to observe. Nevertheless, it should be noted that, as a consequence of the ever-rising level of philosophic work, the Marxist-Leninist philosophers themselves have become conscious of the necessity of making a distinction between politics and propaganda, on the one hand, and technical philosophy, on the other. This sometimes means that the "unity of theory and practice" which is so constantly propagated by the Party becomes, in the mouth of the philosophers, nothing but a phrase.

2. Here are some such works: Weinberger, O.: *Die Sollsatzproblematik in der modernen Logik*. Rozpravy ČSAV, 1959, 9, Berka, K.: *K formulaci sylogismu u Aristotela*. In: Filosofický časopis, Prague (henceforward: FC), 1956, 3, 365–373; Filkorn, V.: *Kausálná logika*. In: Slovenský filozofický časopis (henceforward: SFC), 1958, 2, 95–117, 1959, 3, 209–219, 1959, 4, 327–357 (an important and, as yet, unfinished study); Sus, O.: *O interpretaci Hegelovy estetiky*. In: FC 1958, 6, 795–846. As is evident, they are mainly studies in logic and aesthetics – sometimes in history of philosophy.

3. On his discussion with the Marxist, A. Schaff, see Lobkowicz, N.: *Das Widerspruchsprinzip in der neueren sowjetischen Philosophie*. Dordrecht. 1960. (henceforward: *Widerspruchsprinzip*) p. 6f.

4. M. A. Krąpiec: *Realizm ludzkiego poznania*. Poznań. 1959.

5. At the beginning of 1956 this journal, which published mainly translations of Russian articles, was absorbed by the FC.

6. For example at the end of 1959 we find numerous small articles by A. Kolman: see RP 21, 10; 8, 11; 22, 12; and 21, 1; 9, 2, 1960.

7. Thus, the *"Literární Noviny"* (1956–1957) contains a drawn-out but sometimes sharp discussion on ideology and science.

8. To our knowledge only in Czechoslovakia and in Hungary are these problems more seriously discussed. See Alexits, G., Fenyö, I.: *Matematika és dialektikus materializmus*. Budapest. 1948. Koutský, K.: *Matematika a dialektický materialismus*. Praha. 1952. and: *Některé ideologické a methodologické otázky v matematice*. In: *Sborník I. ideologicko-metodologické konference . . . v Brně*. Praha. 1955 (pp. 20–28). Felber, St.: *Filozofia matematiky*. Bratislava. 1959. and: *Podstata matematiky*. In: SFC 1956, 1, 47–65; Rieger, L.: *O marxistické pojetí matematiky*. In: *Časopis pro pěstování matematiky* 1951, 2, 73–102. The same theme was often treated in reference to B. Bolzano.

9. See M. Machovec: *Stručný přehled dějin filosofie*. Prague. 1956 (p. 44f.).

10. Reprinted in FC 1956, 5, 749–771.

11. Already in 1936 Svoboda had published a small book on Soviet philosophy as well as a translation of Lenin's "Materialism and Empiriocriticism". In 1953 he translated Lenin's "Philosophic Notebooks".

12. Thus, the two Communist poets, St. K. Neumann (1875–1947) and J. Fučík (1903–43), were listed as pre-war philosophers.

13. According to a report of Radio Bratislava (18 December 1959), A. Kolman has been recently named director of the Philosophic Institute of the ČSAV – since the beginning of 1960 he has been a member of the editorial staff of the FC. Dates: A. Kolman, born 6 December 1892 in Prague; professor in Moscow, 23 December

1939; 11 November 1945, professor in Prague. See also *Widerspruchsprinzip* p. 4f.

14. Previously in Slovakia there was only the *"Filozofický odbor Matice slovenskej"*, founded by Št. Polakovič (1941) a Blondelist and follower of Tiso; it published the *"Filozofický sborník Matice slovenskej"*, which appeared until 1947.

15. See the attacks in Nová Mysl 1959, 4, 387–404; 6, 571–577: Tvorba 26 February 1959, p. 207f.; 25 June 1959, p. 614f.; FC 1959, 3, 299–321, 431–436; 5, 643–677; 6, 804–830.

16. See, for example, *Filosofie v dějinách českého národa*. Praha. 1956 (pp. 31 and 253ff.).

17. For the psychology of these "converts" it is interesting to read L. Rieger's autobiographical essay, *Filosofická retrospektiva*. In: FC 1956, 5, 744–749.

18. Kalivoda delivered an address at the Congress for Medieval Philosophy in Louvain (Belgium); he was one of the few Marxists among the many Thomists. See his report in: FC 1959, 3, 462–465.

19. Some representatives of this group became quite respectable, e.g. M. Machovec and L. Tondl.

20. Svoboda, K.: *Antika a česká vzdělanost od obrození do první války světové*. Praha. 1957 – a very interesting book.

21. This theme, which belongs to the philosophy of law, was treated mainly by teachers in the Faculty of Law; see, especially: Houška, J., Kára, K.: *Otázky lidové demokracie v Československu*. Praha. 1957. See also: Slapnicka, H.: *Die Loslösung der tschechischen Rechtswissenschaft vom abendländischen Rechtsdenken*. In: Europa Archiv 1954, 24, 7166ff. and review of Lakatoš: *Otázky lidové democracie v Československa*. (Praha. 1957) In: Ztschrft f. Ostforschung 1958, 2, 298f.

22. Kolman, A.: *Kritický výklad symbolické metody moderní logiky*. Praha. 1948. This study is significant because it appeared long before the Soviet logic-discussion began.

23. Zich, O.: *Lidová přísloví s logického hlediska*. Praha. 1956.

24. Filkorn, V.: *Predheglovská logika*. Bratislava. 1953. A very interesting history of logic up to Hegel, from a Marxist standpoint.

25. See K. Berka: *Der "Beweis durch Heraushebung" bei Galenos*. In: Phronesis 1958, 2, 150–153. This is one of the rare publications by a Czech philosopher in a Western, non-Communist, technical journal. Most of them treat of questions of logic. See also, e.g., O. Weinberger: *Über die Negation von Sollsätzen*. In: Teoria (Lund) 1957, 102–132.

26. *Psychologie d'Ibn Sīnā (Avicenna) d'après son oeuvre Aš-Šifā' éditée et traduite en français par Ján Bakoš*. Ed. de l'Academie tchécoslovaque des sciences. Prague. 1959. 2 vols. J. Bakoš, born in 1890 and habilitated in 1931, is today professor of Semitic philology in Bratislava and member of the SAV.

27. Linhart, J.: *Americký pragmatismus*. Praha. 1949. Russian: Moskva. 1954. Bodnár, J.: *O súčasnej filozofii v USA*. Bratislava. 1956. Russian: Moskva. 1959.

28. The address was first published in Nejedlý's private magazine, *Var* 1950, 1, 1–16. See also, Zd. Nejedlý: *Za kulturu lidovou a národní*. Praha. 1953 (pp. 258–279).

29. See Nejedlý, Zd.: *T. G. Masaryk ve vývoji české společnosti a českého státu*. Praha. 1950. V. Kopecký: *Masaryk a komunisté*. Praha. 1950. Masaryk's "relative progressivity" is justified by his exposure of the "Köninginhofer" and "Grünberger" manuscripts as well as by his courageous bearing in the anti-Semitic demonstrations of 1899.

30. The standard philosophical work on this question is Sirácky, A.: *Klérofašistická ideológia l'udáctva*. Bratislava. 1955.

REFERENCES

31. Originally there was only a "Cabinet for Philosophy" (1953) in the ČSAV; on 1 Jan. 1957 it became a Philosophical Institute. The director was L. Rieger from 1953 to 1958 – later either L. Svoboda or V. Ruml. The Philosophic Institute of the SAV originated in 1946 and was part of the old SAVU. The director has been, almost without interruption, I. Hrušovský, who is, at the same time, the director of the entire Section for Social Sciences of the SAV.

32. It seems that cooperation between the Czech and Slovak institutes has not been too great.

33. This ceased with the Tondl Affair. Then, for the first time, the fanaticism which had been common in *"Nová Mysl"* was introduced into the technical, philosophic journals.

34. See *Widerspruchsprinzip* p. 7f. To the literature quoted there, one might add: Zeman, J.: *Ještě k problémům rozpornosti pohybu*. In: FC 1960, 2, 240–243. The discussion is still going on.

35. This last was always opposed, but not by the philosophers themselves. See, e.g., the comments of the president of the SAV, In: *Vestník Slovenskej akadémie vied* 1959, 1/2, pp. 12–13 and 18–19 (contact with the scientists of the capitalists lands has definite disadvantages; it is a "bad habit").

36. It is V. Filkorn and P. Materna who, above all, have dealt with the question.

37. In so many words, in the resolution of the First Conference on Slovak Philosophy in Bratislava, Nov. 1950. See SFC 1950, p. 82.

38. Thus, K. Kosík (FC 1954, 3, p. 206) relates that there is a wide-spread opinion that Masaryk was no philosopher; this is correct. "But this phrase, taken literally, leads to inattention to the idealistic essence of Masarykism."

39. It is hardly possible to give exact figures. In the FC and SFC we find articles by about 100 authors, about half of whom can be called philosophers. The number of teachers of Marxism-Leninism is, of course, much higher.

L. VRTAČIČ

MARXIST-LENINIST LITERATURE IN JUGOSLAVIA

(1945-1959)

Jugoslav Marxism-Leninism is an interesting field which has hardly been explored up to now. The interest consists in the fact that we find in this country a development which, at least as of 1948 (the break with the Cominform), has been relatively independent of that in the Soviet Union. And this autonomy is such as has hardly been seen either in the other "people's democracies" or in China. Has Marxism-Leninism developed differently under these circumstances than it has in the SU and the other states which are dependent on it? What is this difference? How essential is it? These are among the questions which Sovietology must ask and seek to answer. As a matter of fact, these problems have been little discussed up to the present. No effort is made here to remedy this situation – rather, we wish to offer an introduction to such study by presenting an over-all view of the organization of philosophical activity in Jugoslavia and of Jugoslav philosophic, i.e. Marxist-Leninist, literature from 1945 to 1959.

POLITICAL AND NATIONAL STRUCTURE

In order to have any understanding at all of the phenomena in question, it is essential to have an idea of the specific political and national structure of Jugoslavia. According to the Constitution of 31 January 1946 (the constitutional reform of 13 January 1953 changed the situation once more), Jugoslavia is a *Federation (Federativna narodna republika Jugoslavija =* The Federate People's Republic of Jugoslavia) made up of six "people's republics" (Serbia, Croatia, Slovenia, Bosnia and Herzogovina, Macedonia and Montenegro), an autonomous province (Vojvodina) and an autonomous territory (Kosovo-Metohija) [1]. This enumeration alone shows how closely the Jugoslav Constitution is modelled on that of the Soviet Union, even as regards terminology (see Art. 13 and 22 of the Soviet Constitution of 1936).

The following table gives an idea of the size of these various sections:

Table I: Population

	1948		1953	
	Thousands	%	Thousands	%
Serbia	4,159.4	26.2	4,471.5	26.3
Vojvodina	1,640.8	10.4	1,669.5	9.8
Kosovo-Metohija	727.8	4.6	808.1	4.8
Croatia	3,779.9	23.8	3,936.0	23.2
Slovenia	1,439.8	9.1	1,504.4	8.9
Bosnia-Herzogovina	2,563.8	16.2	2,847.5	16.8
Macedonia	1,153.0	7.3	1,304.5	7.7
Montenegro	377.2	2.4	419.9	2.5
Totals	15,841.7	100.0	16,997.4	100.0

The recognition of the numerous nationalities is in accord not only with the Soviet example but also with the factual situation in Jugoslavia. According to the count made in 1953 (Statistical Yearbook of Jugoslavia 1959, p. 55) there were in Jugoslavia:

Table II: Nationalities

Serbian	7,065,923
Croatian	3,975,550
Slovene	1,487,100
Macedonian	893,247
Montenegrian	466,093
Jugoslav (unspecified)	998,698
"Others"	2,025,173
"Remaining"	18,400
"Unknown"	6,389
Total	16,936,573

The "others" includes Scipetars, Magyars, Turks, Slovaks, Gypsies, Bulgars, Germans, Rumanians, Ruthenians, Ukrainians, Walachians, Italians, Czechs and Russians.

Jugoslavia, then, is thoroughly multi-national. The fact is fully recognized by the party in power and is reflected in a special way in Jugoslav literature, philosophical and other. And there is in this context a surprising equality of the different languages. We do not know of any other Communist country outside of the Soviet Union where so many philosophical writings are published in so many languages at the same time (or almost) as in Jugoslavia. Of course, there is a tendency, in principle and already somewhat in practice, to lump things under the term "Jugoslav",[2] but in the period that interests us the general rule was the maintenance of a multilingual publication of philosophic works.

But from the fact of a federative constitution and the recognition of several languages, should not be drawn the conclusion that the single republics, i.e. nations, enjoy a real autonomy. Just as in the Soviet Union, the *state* is federal but the *party* which rules the state through a personal union is completely monolithic (Art. 6 of the Constitution [3]).

ORGANIZATION

To the federative and multi-national structure of Jugoslavia corresponds a very developed network of institutions which form the framework for research, teaching and publishing in the domain of philosophy. There are, as a matter of fact, three academies, five faculties of philosophy, several philosophic societies and, finally, a large number of publishing houses which publish, along with other things, philosophical works.

ACADEMIES

There are three academies: *Jugoslovenska akademija znanosti i umjetnosti* (Jugoslav Academy of Sciences and Arts) in Zagreb, *Srpska akademija nauka* (Serbian Academy of Sciences) in Belgrade, and *Slovenska akademija znanosti in umetnosti* (Slovene Academy of Sciences and Arts) in Ljubljana. Each of them has a special section for philosophy, viz. for history and the social sciences.

These are institutions which existed before 1945. After the war they expanded their fields of activity (by establishing new institutes) and intensified their research work. This is especially true of the sections for technical sciences. The academies create and preserve the possibility of a continuity of research in all fields. They were reorganized after the war and are again threatened with a reform [4], but they remain the top centres of research. Only these academies were in a position to maintain that continuity which is in general so significant for the harmonious development of a people.

Their value is evident to one who is conscious of the difficulties and dangers to which the continuity of formation in scientific institutions is subject. Such is the situation today in Jugoslavia.

FACULTIES OF PHILOSOPHY

As of 1946 (date of the foundation of universities in Sarajevo and Skopje) Jugoslavia had five universities: Belgrade (Serbian), Zagreb (Croatian), Ljubljana (Slovene), Sarajevo (Bosnian-H.), Skopje (Macedonian), each of which has a faculty of philosophy. In addition, there are such faculties in Novi Sad and Zadar, which belong, respectively, to the universities of Belgrade and Zagreb. A glance at the programs of these seven faculties shows [5] that they teach not only philosophy alone, as is the case in the Soviet Union, but also the other humanities.

From time to time there are conferences (e.g. 10 to 12 January 1956) of these faculties for the discussion of the organization and coordination of teaching [6].

PHILOSOPHIC SOCIETIES

Already in 1951 there was a "Serbian Philosophic Union" *(Srpsko filozofsko društvo)* which had been founded at a congress in Belgrade (23 to 25 March 1951). The "Jugoslav Union for Philosophy and Sociology" *(Jugoslovensko udruženje za filozofiju i sociologiju)* was founded in Novi Sad (9 and 10 November 1956).

PUBLISHING HOUSES

Among the large state-owned publishing houses which regularly publish philosophical works, the following should be named: in Belgrade; *"Kultura"*, *"Prosveta"*, *"Naučna knjiga"*, *"Rad"* (popular); in Zagreb; *"Kultura"*, *"Naprijed"*, *"Matica Hrvatska"*, *"Školska knjiga"*; in Ljubljana; *"Cankarjeva založba"*; in Skopje; *"Kultura"*; in Sarajevo; *"Veselin Masleša"*.

BIBLIOGRAPHY

The main source for general Jugoslav bibliography is the *"Bibliografija Jugoslavije"* which appears fortnightly (up to 1953 it was a monthly).

114

Books and articles are distributed in sections according to a decimal classification. The following sections are of interest for philosophy: 1. *Filozofija*, 1.1. *dijalektički i istoriski materijalizam*, 1.11. *dijalektički materijalizam*, 1.12. *istoriski materijalizam*. In certain instances this division is not followed and all relevant works are grouped under "1. *Filozofija*". For the period 1945–1949 we have only a retrospective bibliography of books (and not articles). This, "*Jugoslovenska bibliografija*" (five volumes), appeared in 1950 and, although the decimal classification is not used, there is a separate section for philosophical works.

Aside from these basic works, there is a series of specialized bibliographies for our domain:

(1) *Bibliografija najvažnije filozofske i sociološke literature na srpskohrvatskom jeziku od* 1945–1957 *godine* (Bibliography of the most Important Philosophic and Sociological Works in Serbo-Croatian in 1945–1957). In: *Jugoslovenski časopis za filozofiju i sociologiju*. 1957, 1, 222–227.

(2) *Popis radova nastavnika Filozofskog fakulteta od oslobodjenja do* 1956. (List of the Works of the Faculty of Philosophy from the Liberation to 1956). In: *Godišnjak Filozofskog fakulteta u Novom Sadu*, 1956, 1, 319–336.

(3) *Zbornik Radova. Knjiga II* (Collection of Works. Book II). Zagreb, Školska knjiga, 1954 (with a list of the works of the Faculty of Philosophy in Zagreb from the liberation to the end of 1953 and a list of the dissertations accepted by this faculty from the liberation to May 1953).

(4) *Univerza v Ljubljani. Biografija in bibliografija univerzitetnih učiteljev in sodelavcev* (University of Ljubljana. Biography and bibliography of the teachers and co-workers of the University). Ljubljana. 1957.

(5) *Pregled izdanja Srpske akademije nauka* 1937/47 (Survey of the Publications of the Serbian Academy of Sciences 1937–47). Beograd, Naučna knjiga. 1948.

(6) *Popis izdanja Jugoslovenske akademije znanosti i umjetnosti u Zagrebu.* 1867–1950 (List of Publications of the Jugoslav Academy of Sciences and Arts in Zagreb. 1867–1950). Zagreb, Jugoslovenska akademija znanosti i umjetnosti, 1951.

(7) Ramovš, P.: *Biblioteka in publikacije Slovenske akademije znanosti in umetnosti v letih* 1938–1951 (Library and Publications of the Slovene Academy of Sciences and Arts for 1938–1951). Ljubljana, Slovenska akademija znanosti in umetnosti, 1952.

JOURNALS

There are two professional philosophical journals in Jugoslavia: *"Filozofs-ki pregled"* (in Serbian – has appeared in Belgrade since 1954) and *"Jugoslovenski časopis za filozofiju i sociologiju"* (as of 1957) which is the publication of the *"Jugoslovensko udruženje za filozofiju i sociologiju"* (Jugoslav Union for Philosophy and Sociology).

However, numerous articles of a philosophical nature also appear in other journals, such as: *"Naša stvarnost"* (in Serbian, Belgrade 1947ff.), *"Pogledi"* (in Croatian, Zagreb 1952ff.), *"Pregled"* (Sarajevo 1954ff.), *"Naša Sodobnost"* (in Slovene, Ljubljana 1953ff.), which was preceded by *"Sodobnost"* before the war. The most prominent of the newspapers which publish philosophic articles are the official paper of the CPJ, *"Borba"* and *"Politika"* (both in Serbian, Belgrade).

THE "CLASSICS"

Below will be found a table *(III)* on Marxist-Leninist literature. The statistics are taken from the *"Jugoslovenska bibliografija"* (1945–49) and *"Bibliografija Jugoslavije"* (as of 1950).

We have considered only those works which are in one of the four national languages, i.e. Serbian, Croatian (Latin script), Slovene and Macedonian. The philosophical works which appeared in the same publishing house in Serbo-Croat at the same time are not listed again [7]. A choice had to be made in the case of psychology and aesthetics where much is to be found which is philosophically uninteresting.

Although we are here interested only in the translations of the "classics" which appeared after the war, it is of interest to note that some were published even before the war [8]. In the first five years after the war the translations were almost exclusively of politico-economic writings. There are exceptions, such as: "Anti-Dühring", "Ludwig Feuerbach" and "Materialism and Empiriocriticism". Only after 1950 was attention paid to translating all the basic works of the "classics" [9]. Stalin's works were publicized even two years after the interruption of friendly relations with the Soviet Union (1948). The *"Bibliografija Jugoslavije"* of 1950 no longer treats him as a "classic" but rather as a Marxist author whose works are included under the rubric, *"Dela ostalih autora"* (Works of Other Authors).

116

The editions of the works of the "classics" are so numerous that only those of the works of Tito can compare with them. The final figures on the edition of a given work can only be reached by including the printings in the various languages, i.e. the four national languages and the languages of the various minorities (e.g. Italian, Hungarian, Rumanian, etc.)[10]. One of the largest printings was that of Stalin's "Questions of Leninism": Serbian (1946) 80,000; (1947) 30,000; Croatian (1946) 40,000; Slovene (1948) 8,000; Macedonian (1949) 7,000. But the average edition is much smaller than this, e.g. Slovene 5,000 and Serbian 10,000.

PHILOSOPHICAL LITERATURE

The Marxist-Leninist literature in the first five years after the Second World War was almost exclusively made up of works of the "classics", as can be seen from Table III below. Of the 32 translations, 30 were of works of Soviet authors, one of a non-Soviet Marxist-Leninist (Mao Tse-tung 1949) and one of a non-Marxist-Leninist (Pre-Socratics 1947).

The Soviet authors involved were (in brackets is given the year of publication and the number of translations): Aleksandrov, G. F. and others (1948), Xasxačix (1948), Gak (1947), Glezerman (1948:2, 1949:2), Iovčuk (1945, 1946), Konstantinov (1946:2), Kornilov (1947:2, 1948), Leonov (1947), Pavlov (1947), Plechanov (1946:4, 1947:2, 1948:2), Rozental' (1949), Svetlov-Ojzerman (1948), Ždanov, A. A. (1947, 1948).

Since 1950 translations of works of Soviet authors are rare: Kol'man (1958), Leonov (1950:3), Psixologija (Kornilov 1950), Rjazanov (1952:2), Rozental' (1952:2). In addition, the translations of the pre-Soviet author, Herzen, should be noted (1949:2, 1951) and, above all, those of Plechanov (1950:2,1951:2, 1952, 1953, 1954:3, 1955:2, 1958, 1959:2).

Non-Soviet Marxists to be met are: Dietzgen (1958), Goldman (1958), Gramsci (1958), Kautsky (1953, 1954:2), Lefèbvre (1957, 1958, 1959), Lukacs (1956, 1959), Mao Tse-tung (1949, 1957), Mehring (1952).

As "others", we find: Adler (1958), d'Alembert (1955), Aristotle (1954, 1958), Arrianus (1958), Bacon (1952), Bergson (1958), Bruno (1959), Campanella (1953), Descartes (1951, 1952, 1957), Diderot (1950), Einstein (1953), Epicurus (1959), Feuerbach (1956:2), Fichte (1956), Freud (1958), Haldane (1951), Hegel (1951, 1952, 1955:2, 1958, 1959), Heraclitus (1954), Holbach (1950), Hume (1956), Kant (1953, 1955, 1956, 1957, 1958), Kung-

L. VRTAČIČ

fu-tse (1958), Lucretius (1951, 1959), La Mettrie (1955), More (1951, 1958), Plato (1955:2, 1957) Politzer (1951:2, 1953), Spinoza (1956, 1959), the pre-Socratics (1947), Wallon (1959), Willwoll (1958), Windelband (1956, 1957).

Table III: Publications

	Translations					Original Literature		
	"Classics"	SU	Marxist	Others	Total	Books	Articles * Journals	Articles * Newspapers
1945–1959	334	55	14	54	123	152	583	353
1945–1949	228	30	1	1	32	9	**	**

* Only articles from 1950–57 are included.
** There should be a retrospective bibliography of articles; but no such is known to us.

118

REFERENCES

1. *Verfassung der Föderativen Volksrepublik Jugoslawien.* Beograd, Službeni list FNRJ, 1947. 134 SS.

2. Tito expressed himself to the Second Plenum of the ZK of the BKJ (Union of Jugoslav Communists) on this question as follows: "For example, the travel documents of our people who leave the country must be *Jugoslav...*" "that it is necessary to gradually do away with this in relation to the nationality of the *Moslems.* *One must allow the people,* when they wish, to be citizens of Jugoslavia without any precision as to nationality *(nacionalno neopredeljeni državljani Jugoslavije)*" (our italics). The 1953 census shows that the *"neopredeljeni"* (unspecified) includes more than only the Moslems – the figures are much too high in comparison with those of 1948.

	Moslems *	*'neopredeljeni'* **
FNRJ	808,921	998,698
VR Serbia	6,586	64,303
AP Vojvodina	1,050	10,537
AG Kosovo-Metohija	9,679	6,241
VR Croatia	1,077	16,185
VR Slovenia	179	1,617
VR Bosnia-H.	788,403	891,800
VR Macedonia	1,560	1,591
VR Montenegro	387	6,424

* Markert, W.: *Jugoslawien (Osteuropa-Handbuch).* Köln/Graz. 1954 (p. 16, Table 5).
** *Statistički godišnjak Jugoslavije* (1959). Beograd (p. 301).

3. *Statut Saveza komunista Jugoslavije.* Beograd. 1957.

4. *Zakon i statut o Jugoslovenskoj akademiji znanosti i umjetnosti.* Zagreb. 1948.

5. Markert *op. cit.* p. 194.

6. Vranicki, P.: *Za bolju organizaciju i ujednačenost nastave.* In: Vjesnik (Zagreb) 17 January 1956.

7. It is question here of the works which appear in Belgrade in Latin and Cyrillic script at the same time. In such cases we are in the presence of a language which is common (under the name Serbo-Croatian) to the Serbians, Croatians, Bosnians-H., and Montenegrans, a common language but which is printed in two different scripts. In the past the Croats used the Latin script while the Serbians used the Cyrillic. Therefore, the Croatians have been able to retain only the script of their own language.

8. The most important of these: "Capital", "Dialectics of Nature", "Anti-Dühring", "Ludwig Feuerbach" and more politico-economic writings (see *Slovenski Poročevalec* 17 April 1959). In Slovenia there were two series, *"Mala biblioteka"* (Little Library) and *"Ekonomska enota"* (Economic Unity) which did translations and took care of the spreading of them (see *ibid.* 5 April 1959).

9. The ZK of the BKJ resolved on 16 April 1959 to publish the complete works of Marx, Engels and Lenin. *"Kultura"* in Belgrade undertook the printing. At the same time, new editions of the single works were supposed to appear. (*ibid.* 17 April 1959).

10. In Hungarian and Rumanian alone there are over 40 works of Marx, Engels and Lenin with a total of 100,000 or more copies (*ibid.* 17 April 1959).

A. BUCHHOLZ

PROBLEMS OF THE IDEOLOGICAL EAST-WEST
CONFLICT *

INTRODUCTION

There can be no doubt as to the fact that the ideological East-West conflict is one of the central problems of our day, and that the way in which it is solved will decidedly influence the structure of the world in the near future. For the solution of this problem the Soviets have set a definite goal for themselves – the only conceivable resolution of the East-West ideological conflict consists in the victory of Communist ideology throughout the world. This demand is so intrinsic to the essence of Soviet ideology that there can be no doubt about it. In view of this fact, the Western thinker must ask himself what real perspectives there are for him in the East-West ideological conflict.

Having excluded the theoretical possibilities that the conflict last "forever", that all life be swept from the earth, or that Soviet ideology conquers through war, the problem is reduced to the following alternatives: either the West becomes Communist or Soviet ideology transforms itself in such a way that the present East-West ideological conflict becomes obsolete. The present work seeks to investigate the second alternative.

The studies which have been made up to now have clearly showed that the investigation of the possibilities of ideological changes in East and West is an extraordinarily vast theme which includes, for example, the following questions: What connection is there between material and ideological changes in the Soviet Union? Where are the developing elements in Soviet philosophy to be found? What are the mutual influences of philosophical currents in East and West? What future, as yet unformulated, problems, could have new ideological consequences?

---

* This paper was composed in May of 1959. In March of 1960 the author had a chance to visit the SU and to discuss some of the limit-problems with Soviet philosophers. Any new perspectives which he gained from these discussions or further reflections on his part, have not been included in this text.

Each of these factors contains a whole series of more specific problems. To work out the whole of the question, one might be tempted to give each problem to a single author for scientific elaboration and then synthesize the results in a mosaic-like, over-all picture. But, aside from the fact that the conditions necessary for such work are lacking, it is doubtful if this procedure would achieve its purpose. Closer consideration shows that all the specific problems are inter-connected and that the essence of the East-West ideological conflict and the means of solving it become directly apparent from the structure of this inter-connection. This gradually-won insight led to the realization of how the complex problem of the East-West ideological conflict could be investigated without, on the one hand, disturbing the above-mentioned structure and, on the other, exceeding the capacities of the single researcher. A road seems open if the following methodological presuppositions are observed:

(1) The problems are not to be "analysed away" but simply recognized for what they are and located in their structural position. Essentially, then, this stage of the work involves solely and simply an investigation of the structural disposition of the problems. This over-all view will serve to throw into relief the key problems in the East-West ideological conflict and to orient future studies to a concentration on those themes which can effectively contribute to an attenuation of the ideological tension.

(2) The second presupposition is based on the fact that it is precisely the posing and formulation of truly scientific problems which is a difficult task and which is the principle weapon of the respective genuine sciences. Since the specialized knowledge of the individual is necessarily limited, this formulation of problems demands the cooperation of scientists from different domains. How to guarantee this cooperation in a free, scientific society is another methodological problem. Among the possibilities are: conferences; long-term work-teams of experts in different fields, who could study the problematic through team-work; or individual researchers who, after interviews with experts in different fields on single aspects, could synthesize, i.e. determine the over-all structure.

But, whatever be the method of organisation, the synthesis accomplished by the individual person will be decisive. Progress in this direction, however, is possible only if one can, from time to time, give a report on the state of our knowledge – this for one's own benefit and that of other researchers. It is in this spirit that in what follows we offer a few of our own reflections on the present state of knowledge on the correlations of the ideological East-West problems.

PRESENT STATE OF DISCUSSION BETWEEN SOVIET AND WESTERN PHILOSOPHY

There is a general impression that, for a long time, there has been no real discussion between Soviet and Western philosophers. This is correct to the extent that direct meetings have been restricted to a few international congresses at which, because of the lack of time, discussions of fundamental questions were not possible.

But the literature contains a rich material on the East-West philosophical discussions. Since the Second World War a great number of critical considerations of Soviet ideology have appeared in the West. Less well known, however, is the fact that there are counter-criticisms from the Soviet side to all the essential Western works on Soviet ideology. They are to be found in book reviews or articles which are aimed at the refutation of Western attacks. There is hardly one argument against Soviet philosophy which is left unanswered. Thus, a critical comparison of the criticisms and counter-criticisms offers important data on the state of the East-West philosophic discussion. In addition to refuting attacks on their own ideology, Soviet philosophers have untertaken the criticism of the major philosophic currents in the West. For about two years now there has been a remarkable activity in this domain and it seems still on to increase. There is, further, a special battle against the so-called "revisionism", which is directed against deviations, in Communistico-socialist lands, from Soviet ideology. At present we know of some 250 publications – Soviet articles, for the most part – which contain elements of the East-West conflict in philosophy. Special studies will have to analyse these discussions more closely. From this, only the most important themes on which these discussions are based, will be retained.

WESTERN ATTACKS ON SOVIET IDEOLOGY METHODOLOGICAL PREREQUISITES

Numerous Western critics of Soviet philosophy restrict their argumentation to the clarification of the methodological presuppositions of Soviet philosophy. Here appears the most significant characteristic of Soviet philosophy – that which is known as "dogmatism" in Western terminology. The dogmatism, the political partisanship and the lack of freedom of discussion of Soviet philosophy are in such basic contradiction to our long scientific and philosophical tradition that all further discussion seems senseless.

The problem of dogmatism, fixity of view-point and freedom of science is, with massive quotations from Western critics, regularly refuted. The same old arguments come back – that no philosophy or science can get along without a point of view, that the Soviet point of view is the only true one because it has historical truth on its side, etc. These arguments can be reduced to certain key problems which are basic to all questions of the East-West ideological conflict.

When, in spite of these basic difficulties, further philosophical discussion is carried on, it is plagued by the premiss – implicit, in most cases – that Soviet philosophy considers itself a science and treats the general principles of logic as independent of ideology. Especially in discussions with foreigners, Soviet philosophers like to stress the scientific character of their philosophy. A well-known Soviet philosopher once formulated this attitude as follows: Dialectical Materialism recognizes everything which results from and is proved by science. Actual discussions with specialists have shown that, as a matter of fact, there is a certain amount of elbow-room as to the scientific character, which is, nevertheless, held within certain bounds which further research will have to determine more closely.

EPISTEMOLOGY

Soviet epistemology is materialistico-realist. A quite serious objection to the theory of knowledge of Dialectical Materialism is that it is as metaphysical, when it comes to essentials, as any other epistemology since it, too, contains postulates which are non-experiential. Soviet philosophy answers this objection by redefining the term "metaphysics". But one is aware that there is no logical proof for the independence and objectivity of the external world and that one must make appeal to "logical necessity". Other objections to the materialist epistemology come from philosophical schools which, like positivism, take a position outside of the "materialism-idealism" opposition or, like existentialism, seek to overcome the "object-subject" dichotomy. These and similar discussions make especially clear the basic points where the materialist theory of knowledge is forced to make a decision.

123

LOGIC

Discussions on logic have become especially frequent in the Soviet Union since Stalin's intervention in the linguistics question (1950) – up to that time, one had been quite content to consider logic as superseded by the dialectic. These discussions have taken on such an amplitude that attacks from the outside are hardly necessary – indeed, the opinions within the Soviet Union were so diverse that a new interpretation was a dire necessity. More recently, the big interest is in logistic and cybernetics, which was earlier rejected as an "American pseudo-science" – until it was seen that it had important practical applications.

THE INFINITY OF MATTER IN SPACE AND TIME

Objections to this thesis of Dialectical Materialism come principally from certain modern astronomical theories and from theories on the conceptual necessity of a *"prima causa"*. These positions are attacked by Soviet philosophers and scientists and refuted by arguments which are drawn from other interpretations of the facts of astronomy and from inferences of "imperfect induction".

THE DIALECTICAL DEVELOPMENT OF MATTER

In this context, Soviet philosophers have to meet, among others, the following objections: that the dialectic is a process of thought but no happening in matter; that one can use the dialectic to describe natural phenomena but cannot explain their causes with it; that there are numerous cases where qualitative changes are preceded by no previous quantitative development; that the appearance of life cannot be explained without an appeal to a higher principle, etc. Examination of the Soviet counters to these arguments permits a closer determination of the point where scientific possibilities are confounded with ideologically subjective norms.

DETERMINISM

Dialectical Materialism's doctrine to the effect that all events on earth are strictly determined has given opportunities to various critics, many of whom, however, do not make a sufficient distinction between "mechanical" and "Dialectical" Materialism. But this question has become urgent because of quantum mechanics and there have been many Soviet discussions devoted to it.

Another rebuke to materialist determinism comes in the problems dealing with free will, responsibility, duty, etc. In proportion to the importance of this problem, we find less discussion with Western critics on related questions than on the other problems. This is due to Soviet ideology's general underestimation of the problem of the person and, further, to certain basic difficulties which these questions pose for Dialectical Materialism. But there are extremely complex argumentations offered which try to explain free will and responsibility as products of psychic determinism.

LAWS OF NATURE AND SOCIETY

Dialectical Materialism's position is characterized by the fact that it claims that human society develops according to laws which are qualitatively, it is true, but not essentially, different from the laws of nature. This raised a veritable storm among Western critics. It is pointed out that it is not possible to infer the necessity of social laws from the working of the laws of nature, as Diamat would have it; that, in distinction to the development of nature, human history is a spiritual event; that Diamat denies the role of personality in history; that ethical and political goals are confused with laws, etc. All these criticisms find Soviet answers. Comparative analysis of Soviet answers shows with special clarity the points where scientific demonstration slides into fixity of viewpoint.

THE DEVELOPMENT OF MODERN SOCIETY

Almost half of the written contributions to the East-West ideological conflict have to do with discussions on the Soviet theses as to the class-bound character of society, the consequent absolute necessity of the proletarian revolution, and the destiny of all of mankind in Communism. Western objections are, among others: the Marxist law according to which the proletarian revolution depends on the capitalistico-industrial level of a country and, therefore, must break out first in the more highly developed countries, has been confirmed neither in the SU nor anywhere else; in opposition to the primitive demand for an elimination of class-conflict, the SU has developed a new class-structure; in the Soviet Union we find an extreme form of governmental capitalism; the Communist attempt to free man by eliminating the state has ended in absolutism and slavery; a consequent "dialectic of history" requires that Communism be replaced by another social form if historical development is not to "stagnate". Further, it can be shown that modern capitalism in no way acts according to the laws prophesied by Historical Materialism – the tension between the proletariat of early capitalism and the "exploiters" has been attenuated by social measures, cooperation, etc.; a new middle class has arisen; economic crises can be prevented, to a large extent, by closely observing the market and by governmental measures; social progress can be made without revolution, the example being the development of Swedish socialism; social development is conditioned by numerous psychological factors, among which the opposition between the "haves" and "have-nots" is of secondary importance; etc.

Even though these Western arguments against Historical Materialism are supported by pregnant examples from science and practical life, Soviet philosophy has not left one unanswered. A great activity is deployed in this context. There are not only books and articles on this question but also frequent conferences. Comparative analysis of the Soviet counter-criticisms shows that recourse is always made to certain definite examples and that ideological evaluation of Soviet philosophy is easier in reference to the social sciences than in the realm of the natural sciences.

SOVIET ATTACKS ON WESTERN PHILOSOPHIC TENDENCIES

Alongside Soviet philosophy's rejection of Western attacks on Dialectical and Historical Materialism, we find an effort to "demolish" Western philosophical theories. This active battle is justified by the fact that Dialectical Materialism is the "only scientific philosophy" and that Western philosophers hinder mankind on the road to Communism. It is granted that "bourgeois" philosophy can contain elements of value, but there is no philosophy except Diamat which is totally to be retained.

Of course, the arguments brought against Western philosophies are quite mixed in with the positions taken in the rejection of Western attacks on Diamat. Nevertheless, these discussions offer some perspectives of their

126

own. One comes to learn Western philosophy as reflected in the Soviet mirror and, further, Soviet philosophy finds itself forced to take a stand on questions which Dialectical Materialism has considered little or not at all. We find comprehensive Soviet "rejection" of the following Western philosophical currents: positivism, especially in relation to modern physics; pragmatism as the specifically Anglo-Saxon philosophy; logistic, semantics and cybernetics, from which certain elements are taken into Diamat; existentialism in its German, French and Italian forms; neo-Kantianism and critical realism; depth-psychology, psychometrics and other Western psychologico-medical theories; the sociological theory of "social mobility" and that of "social stratification", "psychosociology", etc. – great attention is paid to the fight against Christianity but the arguments have hardly changed since the time of Feuerbach and Engels; neo-Thomism, little noticed for a long time, has been strongly attacked since the International Congress of Philosophy in Venice. On the other hand, Asiatic philosophies are handled carefully, the materialist elements being put to the fore. There is a special activity in the field of aesthetics which is due to the attacks, occasioned by more frequent cultural exchanges, of Western critics, on "socialist realism".

The main objection to be made against Soviet philosophers in their disputes with Western philosophers is not the criticism itself. Such criticisms and counter-criticisms fill the history of philosophy. What Soviet philosophy lacks, however, is the effort to get to know and understand the true nature of other philosophical currents.

THE CONFLICT WITH REVISIONISM

Under "revisionism" is included any deviation from the ideological line established in the Soviet Union. These take the form, for the most part, of criticisms of Soviet philosophy by the comrades in the popular democracies and the West. The social-democrats who appeal to Marx are also included. While Soviet criticism of philosophy in the West has primarily a strictly formal character, Soviet philosophers are fierce with the members of their own clan. Mutual incriminations form the substance of these polemics and a recent Soviet book carried the title, "Revisionism – the Greatest Danger". A frequent Soviet accusation is that of dogmatism. And this is quite strange in view of the fact that it is the revisionists who accuse the Soviets of dogmatism because of their refusal to see the historical changes which necessitate a change of doctrine. At the same time, since the "revisionists" claim to be real Marxists they bolster their standpoint with quotations from the "classics", especially with Lenin's statement to the effect that Diamat must develop with historical evolution in general. This recourse to the "classics" is termed dogmatism by the Soviets. A classic example is Tito, who points out that the Soviet leaders have set aside that basic tenet of Marxism-Leninism which deals with the dying-away of the state and, in its place, have set up dogmatism, absolutism and bureaucratism. To the Soviets, this is all dogmatism. It would be exaggerating to try to maintain that all the points of conflict between the Soviets and revisionism have correlatives in the conflict of the Soviets with philosophy in the West. But it is possible that a comparative study of the problematic of the revisionism conflict would vouchsafe some valuable insights into the East-West ideological conflict. The very points which the "revisionists" are trying to "revise" are those where Soviet philosophy feels least comfortable.

Essential to the Soviet conflict with Western philosophy are questions of scientific procedure, etc., while the fight with revisionism is centred on the principle of "party-mindedness". Every deviation is met with recourse to this principle, by saying that deviations hurt the cause and aid the enemy. Especially evident at this point is the imprint of subjective norms on Soviet philosophy.

METHODOLOGICAL CONCLUSIONS FROM THE DISCUSSIONS

The investigation of the present-day state of the East-West philosophical discussion involves a vast problematic – one could write a whole book on each of the specific questions involved. But the work we have in mind here cannot possibly decide on the veracity of all the discussions, rather it aims at bringing to the fore the structural and methodological peculiarities of Soviet philosophy as these are revealed in the East-West discussion, in order to conclude as to the limits and value of further discussions. Although this work remains to be completed, there are some evident points.

A comparative analysis of the discussions makes it possible to detect in Soviet ideology a mixture of science and subjective norms. It doesn't matter which question is chosen, there is always a scientific demonstration behind which we find the application of principles which are not derived from the scientific material but which, in the final analysis, lie in the ethical domain. In this way, all the essential decisions of the individual are ideologically predetermined.

Another opening is the fact that Soviet philosophy has no theory of value. Although recent writings in "Communist morality" make some steps in this direction, this constitutes a large chink in Soviet ideological armour. It is from the relation of science to subjective norms that the Soviet conception of freedom is constructed. Freedom is "insight into necessity"; and necessity is dictated, in its turn, by science and Soviet ideology. According to this version, there is true freedom only for the adherents of the ideology of Diamat.

The relationship of science, philosophy and theory of values seems to be a fruitful ground for discussion with the Soviets; for, to the extent that the structure of a system becomes more vast, it seems that the necessity of some sort of evaluation is increasingly felt. The question as to the distribution of science, philosophy and values in the various special domains will, it seems, be interesting enough to both sides to permit real discussion and, consequently, a progressive clarification of terms.

If one asks the Soviets what problems they think would be ideal for East-West discussion, they propose the following themes, for example: cooperation in the fight for peace; peaceful coexistence; banning of nuclear weapons, etc. Western critics refuse these themes because, it is said, they are simple propaganda moves. It remains to be seen to what extent such questions can lead to the discussion of basic ethical issues and, therefore, to some progress in the East-West ideological conflict.

THE INTERPLAY OF WESTERN AND EASTERN INTELLECTUAL CURRENTS

Due to the relative independence of the two blocs and the closed character of Soviet ideology, there is little reason to speak of any influence of the one on the other. The main influence of the Soviet view on the West seems to be that of engendering a reaction in which the West becomes conscious of the value of its views by comparing them with those of the SU. It seems that Western views should have quite an effect in the East, but objective observations of Soviet development and reports of Russian tourists should make us wary of overestimating the drawing-power of our views.

This minimal contact should, it seems, lead to the conclusion that a peaceful solution of the East-West ideological conflict is less likely than an elimination of one by the other. But there are points of contact and there seems to be, in the East, a tendency toward a more open attitude and, in the West, an effort to consolidate. If this is true, then it is obvious that we must concentrate on those points which offer some promise of admitting agreement. A presupposition, in any case, seems to be that each side realize that understanding the other is a good preparation for being understood by him. If each tries to find the worthwhile points in the doctrine of the other, then something like a base of discussion will be established from which further and more disputed questions can be attacked.

THE PROBLEM OF THE FURTHER DEVELOPMENT OF DIALECTICAL MATERIALISM

Concrete discussions with adherents of Dialectical Materialism have shown that they are willing to take up the discussion of views only if these are posed from the point of view of Diamat. Therefore, it is a methodological question of finding those questions which are little discussed in Diamat (but, nevertheless, are there) and which open out into fields which Diamat has not explored.

THE WAY TO THE LIMIT-QUESTIONS OF DIALECTICAL MATERIALISM

The studies proposed in the first section of this paper will allow the Western researcher to establish the exact distribution of subjective norms in Diamat and, at the same time, its limits. From here, can be found those questions which are seriously discussed in the West and which are not seriously discussed, but should be, in Diamat. Convincing Soviet philosophers that these "empty domains" are real problems is, of course, no easy task and presupposes the thorough elaboration of all the elements by experts in the matter. The delimitation of these fields will provide the raw materials for further discussions and, at the same time, indicate the probable directions in which Diamat will develop. Among such domains, the following seem obvious: the question of the meaning of life; the problem of death; intuitive knowledge; and all the questions of the individual and his problems.

THE BALANCE-PROBLEM OF SOVIET IDEOLOGY

The fact that scientific and social questions almost completely dominate contemporary Soviet philosophy and that questions as to the place of the person are given almost no consideration is significant for determining the weak and strong points of Soviet philosophy. Thus, it is obvious that contact can be made with the supporters of Diamat on questions dealing with the person, for which they have no ready-made answers, more easily than on questions dealing with the nature of matter, where they have an entire "bible" of answers. Further, this imbalance of Diamat is significant for its future development. For further stress on the person is bound, it seems, to be accompanied by significant shifts in the dialectico-materialist chapters on matter and determinism.

THE RELATIONSHIP OF MATERIALISM AND RELIGION

The fundamental point of discord between the East and West lies in the very radical contradiction posed by the Soviets between materialism and religion. The solution, it seems, must come by way of an inference of the essence of religion from Diamat; no easy task – but one which seems to be made at least feasible by certain *lacunae* in Diamat's theory of knowledge. The epistemology of Diamat is thoroughly rationalist and completely realist – there is no consideration of the problems of intuition, internal experience, meditation, the "I", the transcendence of knowledge, etc. If, within the discussions, Soviet philosophy could be brought to recognize the serious-ness of these problems, then the above inference seems completely possible.

CONCLUSION

Should Soviet philosophy take a considered stand on the questions of transcendence and religion, this would entail a fundamental transforma-tion in the Eest-West philosophical oppostion. But all human experience tends to show that a considered stand is the first step toward a genuine knowledge of the true nature of the world. Such a development would, ob-viously, be the end of Diamat as we know it and, eventually, the end of the ideological East-West conflict.

INDEX OF NAMES

INDEX OF SUBJECTS